# THE POWER OF PAPER

## OF PAPER

A HISTORY,
A FINANCIAL ADVENTURE,
AND A WARNING

*Also by the author*

THE PRIME MINISTERS OF CANADA

OLYMPIC VICTORY

LEOPARD IN THE AFTERNOON

THE MAN-EATER OF PUNANAI

SINDH REVISITED

JOURNEY TO THE SOURCE OF THE NILE

HEMINGWAY IN AFRICA

WOOLF IN CEYLON

# THE POWER
# OF PAPER

## A HISTORY,
## A FINANCIAL ADVENTURE,
## AND A WARNING

CHRISTOPHER
ONDAATJE

HarperCollins*PublishersLtd*

*The Power of Paper*
© 2006 by Christopher Ondaatje.
Foreword © 2006 by Peter C. Newman
All rights reserved.

Published by HarperCollins Publishers Ltd

First edition

HarperCollins books may be purchased for educational, business,
or sales promotional use through our Special Markets Department.

HarperCollins Publishers Ltd
2 Bloor Street East, 20th Floor
Toronto, Ontario, Canada
M4W 1A8

*www.harpercollins.ca*

Library and Archives Canada Cataloguing in Publication

Ondaatje, Christopher
The power of paper : a history, a financial adventure, and a
warning / Christopher Ondaatje.

ISBN-13: 978-0-00-200860-0
ISBN-10: 0-00-200860-2

1. Paper money—History. 2. Power (Social sciences). 3. Ondaatje,
Christopher. 4. Capitalists and financiers—Biography. I. Title.

HG353.O53 2007    332.4'04409    C2006-906127-0

9 8 7 6 5 4 3 2 1

Designed and typeset by Libanus Press, Marlborough, Wiltshire
Reprographics by Lyndale PhotoGraphic Ltd, Devon
Printed and bound by Butler & Tanner in the United Kingdom

*For the staff of
Loewen Ondaatje McCutcheon & Company Limited, 1970–1988:
because without you it wouldn't have been half as much fun.*

# PHOTOGRAPHIC ACKNOWLEDGEMENTS

The author and publishers express their thanks to the following sources for permission to reproduce illustrated material. In the event that any omissions have occurred, proper acknowledgements will be made in future editions.

Genève, Bibliothèque Publique et universitaire, P. Gen. Inv 50. Photo Viviane Siffert, Faculté des lettres, Université de Genève: 30

Yale Babylonian Collection: 32, 33, 64, 65

British Library: 34

National Archaeological Museum, Athens: 35

Getty Images / Hulton Archive: 36, 37, 49, 51, 63, 73, 79, 97, 143, 146, 166, 196, 204

Getty Images: 38, 98, 186, 207

AFP / Getty Images: Front jacket, 219

Time Life Pictures / Getty Images: 84, 107, 125, 135, 174, 197, 222

Beinecke Rare Book and Manuscript Library, Yale University: 88, 100

Frans Hals Museum, The Netherlands: 94

Ondaatje Foundation: 119, 160, 162, 163, 164, 168, 176, 187, 190, 191, 195

Stephen Roman: 129

Peter C. Newman: 139

Library and Archives Canada PA 131992, PA 171758: 141 (detail), 144

Jack Cockwell: 183

# CONTENTS

ACKNOWLEDGEMENTS                                                      9

INTRODUCTION BY PETER C. NEWMAN                                      11

CHAPTER 1   *Riches from Rags: The Uses of Paper*                    27

CHAPTER 2   *Financial Instruments: The Paper Economy*              61

CHAPTER 3   *Student of Finance: Dreams about Paper*               103

CHAPTER 4   *Investing in Canada: A New World of Paper*            131

CHAPTER 5   *The Pagurian Story: An Empire of Paper*               155

CHAPTER 6   *Warnings from History: The Abuse of Paper*            193

SOURCES OF QUOTATIONS                                              223

BIBLIOGRAPHY                                                       227

INDEX                                                              231

# AUTHOR'S ACKNOWLEDGEMENTS

My chief reason for writing *The Power of Paper*, and especially for publishing it now, is a sense of alarm at what is happening in the world economy. In my view, the present abuse of paper threatens to destabilize civilization.

*The Power of Paper* is not an autobiography, but it does of course lean on my own financial career and subsequent experience, from the late 1940s until now. As a compulsive diarist and journal-keeper, I kept detailed notes and records of all that happened to me from the moment I arrived penniless in Canada in April 1956 to the day in December 1988 when I became disillusioned with finance, sold my companies, and left the financial scene forever. These documents, as with any archive, act as a reality check on my memories of a story that with all its ups and downs, successes and setbacks, euphoria and depression, still seems to me like a fairy tale.

Nevertheless, in putting the book together, I had some valuable help delving into the four or five historical millennia of paper and finance. I am grateful to Dinny Gollop and Joanna Macnamara, loyal assistants, for their research enabling me to reconstruct the story. Thanks too to the financial analyst William R. Sumpton, who worked with me in Canada for nearly 17 years; he helped me to put chapter five, "The Pagurian story", into perspective, deciphering the contemporary analyses written by some of the best known and respected of financial commentators, including Peter C. Newman, who has written the introduction to this book.

Once again, I am grateful to Andrew Robinson for his expert opinion and guidance in forcing me to cut down a long and unwieldy manuscript. I am certain now that he was right in insisting that I publish only the most relevant of the more personal aspects of my own story, mainly where they relate to the story and lessons of Pagurian. In the end we both felt that it was important to concentrate on the history of paper in its widest context, leading to the sombre warning in chapter six.

A final thank you goes to Michael Berry and Michael Mitchell who managed the book's design and production. We had a lot of fun together digging up illustrations to fit the text. It would have been difficult to create this book without them.

# INTRODUCTION

When I read the intriguing pages that follow I was struck by how closely the author of this remarkable book resembles the fabled Scheherazade, who spun her tales for the legendary King of Samarkand through a Thousand and One Nights. Like Christopher Ondaatje, she feared for her life, not because it was threatened but because it might be revealed. He is a careful hombre, is our Christopher, and *The Power of Paper* is as close as he intends to wade into the quick-sands of autobiography—which is to say, not very far. This is a shame, because the first-person story of his unscripted life is a tall tale that deserves to be told. He did it all, his way, and it's a magnificent saga worthy of a Korda film. Meanwhile, the quest for the real Ondaatje—The English Patron, not that other younger brother, known for *The English Patient*—continues.

This introduction is a modest attempt to probe his singular life and boisterous times, not because I am nosy but because he has become a public presence who arouses great curiosity by his twin preoccupations of giving away most of his world-class fortune, and writing extraordinarily original books—this is his tenth—that shine searchlights into history's and geography's darker, inadequately explored corners.

Our destinies are dictated by time and circumstance. "One cannot divine nor forecast the conditions that will make for happiness," concluded the poet Willa Cather. "One only stumbles on them by chance in a lucky hour, at the world's end, and holds fast to the days."

"Nonsense!" I can hear Christopher respond, his patrician body exploding like a jack-in-the-box out of its chair, the tanned, aquiline face creased with annoyance. "You make your own luck."

I don't know whether he actually said that, but it constitutes a valid summary of his work ethic. You don't exchange pleasantries with the elder Ondaatje brother, or make the kind of small talk that titled Englishmen, blowing through their moustaches, indulge in to pass the time of day. Friends and foes alike who deal with Christopher find themselves facing an energy force comparable to that of an early combustion engine in permanent overdrive, lacking a governor or muffler. The James Watt metaphor is apt because his jolting discourse is driven by an inexhaustible head of steam. He talks at a rapid, almost incomprehensible clip except when he is sharing a confidence. Then he lowers his voice, glances around the room, and whispers cryptic asides, like a Cold War spy divulging the address of his East Berlin safe house. One interviewer described his speech pattern as "an extraordinary, unregulated experience, stumbling in a rush of syllables, at times almost shrieking with urgency." That may be true but his bark is more deadly than his bite. He has the knack of making even his oft-told tales about old cricket matches sound like deadly jousts and may well be London's most compelling conversationalist.

His pedigree is Old World Upper Crust but that's of little account, since in this topsy-turvy twenty-first century, you are only required to look and behave like some distant regal. Sir Christopher Ondaatje, Commander of the Order of the British Empire and a Knight of the Realm, who was anointed recently by London's authoritative *Spectator* as "one of the most remarkable men of our times" fits the bill. He spent his formative glory years in Ceylon, earned his outsize fortune in Canada, and now roosts in a splendidly appointed flat in the upper reaches of Sloane Square. His baronial, 93-acre country seat, Glenthorne, on the north Devon coast, which took ten years to build following the laying of its foundations in 1825, ranks among the most elegant, restored late Regency manor houses in Great Britain. Its driveway is three miles long and its 29 rooms burst with the largest private collection of Sri Lankan antiquities.

Like those of us who have been torn from our youthful roots, he has spent most of his frantic lifetime searching for security and stability in foreign venues, finding safe haven in causes to follow and disciples to emulate—either through his faith in them, or, as these relationships matured, their faith in him. At 17, when his alcoholic father dragged the family into bankruptcy and divorce courts, he was forced to leave Blundell's, the British public school in Tiverton, Devon that had imbued him with social graces. In his teenage fury, he vowed never to be that vulnerable again: he would pledge his loyalty to those who earned it, and return its benefits many times over. Being suddenly penniless never stopped him acting like a prince.

His life became a series of commercial triumphs that left him wealthy beyond his most grandiose ambitions. Despite his quixotic turns and passionate nature, he possessed a remarkable interior gyroscope that kept him on a level course, re-inventing himself with each new situation. He beat the odds by moving beyond the oft-quoted Darwinian admonition about "survival of the fittest"—a maxim that was actually coined by the British ethicist Herbert Spencer at a different time in a different context. Instead, Ondaatje adhered to the precise text of the evolution master's theory which called for survival of the most adaptable. Now, *this* was a maxim he could live by. That the nimble always prevail is an Ondaatje catechism, if there ever was one.

Fast on both feet and terminally adaptable, he found his métier in an unbridled form of capitalism that required unconditional belief unhindered by any sense of sin—like Canada's Inuit must have felt about sex before the missionaries came. Apart from creating fortunes for its successful practitioners, he regarded capitalism as a system dedicated to socializing anarchy and bringing profitable order out of disarray.

These were his articles of faith and he successfully exploited that belief system when negotiating the business deals that fuelled his professional life. In the context of his improbably bullish financial career, Ondaatje did not shy away from casting himself as a self-confessed predator. One could easily imagine him stalking a leopard—his favourite beast of the jungle and a furry killing machine which thrives on its predator instincts.

The big cats had mesmerized him since his youthful journeys from Taprobane, a tiny island off Ceylon's south coast, to the arid jungles of the southeast. He has identified with them ever since. "Leopards are born predators, the most ruthless of animals, most hated, most glamorous, most elusive—the only animals, besides man, that kill not just in self-defence, but for the sake of killing," he enthuses. "But I love them. I have always identified with predators." He endows modern corporations with the beasts' savage ethic, noting that in business—as in the jungle—"there are only winners and losers. No half way. You are either predator or prey. Since I didn't want to end up as prey, I became a predator." His 1991 inner journey, *The Man-Eater of Punanai*, remains his most emotionally evocative book.

Having made his fortune in the bitches' brew of high finance, he determined to seek absolution in philanthropy and authorship. He has found great pleasure in both pursuits, and has succeeded admirably in carving out a burnished new persona. Like some golden homing pigeon clutching bank drafts in its claws, he has been drawn to circumstances that inspired him to share his wealth with worthy causes, most of them having to do with the arts, and all of them investigated with the same tough criteria he used to judge risky investments. "I won't give money to anything in which I don't get involved. I am not going to give money away just to satisfy somebody else's ego." By rough calculation his philanthropy has cost him over $60 million over the past decade. As one observer of his generosity has remarked, he has had enough wings of museums and galleries named after him (in London, Halifax, Toronto and Bermuda) to start an airline. The £2.5 million Ondaatje donated to London's National Portrait Gallery in 1996 was the prototype for his strategic philanthropy. It was exactly the figure (and the timing) that the gallery's director Charles Saumarez Smith required from private sources to spring free Heritage Lottery funds of £12 million which allowed him to build its prestigious new wing that was named after Ondaatje. Still, it took the Gallery nearly five years to acknowledge his gift and name him one of its trustees.

"There's a different set of rules in England for someone like me who is a free enterpriser from North America who then settles."

Significantly, it was the Queen who officially opened the Ondaatje wing, and therein lies a tale. In 2002, when Conrad Black, then the proprietor of London's *Daily Telegraph*, was elevated to a peerage, he was forced much against his will by Jean Chrétien, then the country's prime minister, to surrender his citizenship, since under an archaic legal amendment Canadians were forbidden to accept foreign titles. A year later, when Ondaatje was offered a knighthood, he declared that he would accept it only if he did not have to surrender his Canadian citizenship. After the announcement he happened to be at a party in Fort Belvedere, hosted by Galen Weston for his wife Hilary, that was attended by the Queen. "After dinner," Ondaatje recalls, "Valda and I got up, and the Queen made her way to where we were standing. Before I could even say 'Your Majesty . . .' she grabbed both my hands and asked whether I had heard from the Canadian Prime Minister—still Jean Chrétien."

When he said that he hadn't, she replied, "Let me tell you he has certainly been in touch with me. My advice to you is to do nothing and let me handle it my way." And that was the end of it. "They let it happen for me. I feel more Canadian now than ever," he purrs. There have many instances of his philanthropy, such as the £1.6 million he donated to the Royal Geographical Society, the £1.4 million he gave to Blundell's, his British alma mater, and the $35 million foundation he established to further "the development of learning and international understanding", as well as donations to the Somerset County Cricket Club, the Royal Ontario Museum, the Art Gallery of Nova Scotia, the Chester Playhouse, Lakefield College School, Pearson College, Dalhousie University and Toronto's Hospital for Sick Children.

Having been a life-long Conservative, his most unusual gift was the £2 million he subscribed in 2003 to assist British Prime Minister Tony Blair, which ranked him as one of the most generous Labour Party contributors. His reason was not so much the attraction of the Socialists as the destructive manner in which he had been treated by the old-line Tories: "I gave quite a lot of money to the Conservatives, and they just took it in an arrogant fashion, as if it were their due," he complains. "They weren't interested in me, or anybody like me. I am sick to death of being beaten down, called a foreigner, and used with bigotry."

Whenever Christopher and I share a meal, the soup plates have barely been cleared before he launches into one of his wonderful rants, and I quickly resurrect a thought from that old scoundrel, Friedrich Nietzsche: "One must have chaos in oneself to give birth to a dancing star." Ondaatje qualifies on both counts. One recent example of our post-soup conversation: well, not really conversation, but a jarring soliloquy from Christopher:

> Today we have a world situation where provinces, govern-
> ments, states, corporations, and individuals are enormously
> in debt. In fact there is probably no possibility of this debt
> ever being repaid. Governments have to raise money just to
> pay the interest on their loan. The only way to repay it is with
> a lesser dollar or a lesser pound. Wars are inflationary and
> this Iraqi war is going to cost America and England a lot of
> money which they cannot afford. The welfare state in both
> countries is either bankrupt or horribly, horribly in debt, so
> the only way out is to continue to print money. My estimate
> is that within ten years, the purchasing power of the dollar
> and the pound will be only 10 per cent of what it is now.
> Guaranteed. *Guaranteed, 10 per cent of what it is in ten
> years*. It may even happen within five years. Actually it's a
> serious problem. If there is a major economic meltdown,
> there will be a banking crisis, which is one of the things that
> happened in the Depression. It could easily happen again—
> in which case it will hasten everything I've said. Wars are
> amazing things. They forgive a lot of ills, paper over the

cracks and give the opportunity to start again. So therefore suddenly if there is a financial crisis which threaten bank failures and the existence of other institutions governments will make some extraordinary judgments to protect the state and to protect our way of life. In England they'll close the bank doors in one second just as they did in the United States during the Depression. Something like that could easily happen within the next five years. That's why we need another visionary like Maynard Keynes.

Amen. Such end-of-civilization discourses before the main course are all very well, but they don't leave much room for dessert.

The passion of his conversations plays to Ondaatje's current, and one assumes final, incarnation, as an agitator and author who views the world with the eyes of a seasoned—and troubled—mountaineer. Perhaps his apocalyptic frame of mind is partly the legacy of being on the ground and making discoveries that will require minor but not irrelevant changes in the world's known geography.

In what must have seemed like a gamble at the time, Ondaatje has devoted most of his energies in the past decade to vindicating and retroactively widening the scope of the original Victorian explorers, the subjects of his vintage books. In the early 1970s, a chance reading of Victorian adventurer Captain Sir Richard Francis Burton's biography, *The Devil Drives* written by Fawn Brody, reoriented his career. "This," Ondaatje decided, "was the life I should have led". (And no, he wasn't referring to Sir Richard's unexpurgated translation of *The Book of the Thousand Nights and a Night*, or the infamous *Kama Sutra*.) One of Burton's greatest adventures was his journey with John Hanning Speke into the perilous heart of equatorial Africa to search for the source of the Nile, which he and subsequent expeditions determined was that continent's greatest inland body of water, Lake Victoria. After he moved to England in the mid-1990s, Ondaatje literally followed Burton's footsteps, wading through every swamp, jungle, dried riverbed and bog—possibly the only person alive today to have followed all of the original Victorian explorers' routes.

While he admired the man, he questioned the resulting theory. In 1996, Christopher embarked on a three-month, 10,000-km expedition that ultimately revised the long-held belief that the Nile originated in Lake Victoria. "Christopher Ondaatje has made some unexpected but fascinating discoveries", declared Lord Selborne, president of the Royal Geographical Society at the time. Ondaatje's book *Journey to the Source of the Nile* sold over 70,000 copies and established his literary reputation. His *Hemingway in Africa*, in which he retraced the author's two safaris through Kenya, Tanzania and Uganda, is my favourite. (Here again, he was drawn to the subject by Hemingway's famed allegory of the leopard's dried and frozen carcass found on a high ledge of Mount Kilimanjaro, Africa's highest mountain.)

The current volume, which he swears will be his last, is the most daunting of his writings because he tackles new territory. In six compelling chapters, he meticulously traces the history of man through the evolving uses of paper and the grandiose games played with it by past and present civilizations—games, for which we are about to pay the piper. The entire text is persuasive but his final section transports readers into essential territory. His chapter titled, "Warnings from history: the abuse of paper", is as significant a piece of economic writing as I have read. It is relevant to anyone who takes business, investments, economics, the future, our irreversible destinies—all that and more, at all seriously. He documents his startling assumption that the impending collapse of global capitalism presents a greater threat than global warming. "Painting makes paper valuable, but writing makes it powerful," he believes. Indeed it does as we follow Christopher Ondaatje's authoritatively researched paper trail. The book takes off every time the author interjects himself into the drama he is describing, such as his epiphany when he fully realizes the awesome power endowed to paper by the monetary values ascribed to it.

If there is a fault in his text, it is his habit of making his career appear more accidental than it was. Throughout his business career—and in this book—Ondaatje portrays himself as just hanging around, grasping unexpected opportunities. In fact, he had a finely honed sixth sense for popping up in the midst of the action. Despite his insistence that he has remained a fortunate *innocente* who just happened to be at the right place at the right time, doing the right thing—I prefer his more substantive claim that he made his own luck. It was, of course, not just being there that counted, but his ability to seize opportunities and run with them on all those occasions that became the defining moments of his professional life.

Since I happen to be Canadian by adoption (just like Christopher, except that Jews rank much higher on the scale of "Not Wanted on Voyage"), I am well aware how much *chutzpah* was required for him to perform the corporate derring-do that characterized his intuitive leaps into the world of Canadian business. Bay Street's wise men—among whom Christopher gained both respect and notoriety—pay little attention to weather; they bet on climate. ("Climate follows predictable patterns; weather is notoriously temperamental.") His was an uncanny sense of timing. He could spot a change in the wind or the shadings of the sky, read political entrails, and switch direction, or make a flash move he had been delaying for two years. He seldom missed the early signals of an approaching market downturn. In 1969, for example, he abruptly sold all his corporate investments just weeks before a major market slump, and repeated that canny tactic in 1981 and 1987. He kept all his companies debt free ("Those who run companies burdened by debt are not working for themselves, but for the banks.") and never purchased more than 50 per cent of any company, no matter how attractive a takeover target it might be. ("If I had, why would the original management work for me?")

Canada's financial establishment is an uptight universe—perhaps hunting preserve is a more suitable description—that operates on perpetuating its status quo through envy. Ondaatje provided the perfect target—as, incidentally, I did—both of us being and remaining certified outsiders, not exactly loved for besting our peers at their own paper games. He, in corporate finance; I, in books.

In one of our many conversations, Christopher summed up the main reason for his success: "It never occurred to me that I might fail." That is not the Canadian way. You assume you're going to fail, or the Presbyterian God will get you.

Ondaatje's claims to be the ultimate outsider—with his olive skin, aristocratic bearing, a self-confidence that bordered on arrogance and an absence of personal resources—were well founded. He came to Canada in 1956, landing at Montreal as a stranger in a strange land. His first sight of the wintry foreign shore that would be his home was best caught in his own words: "I stood with the other passengers in the shelter of the open shed and gazed miserably at the bleak prospect of Montreal's Pier 26—my first view of Canada after eight days of the Atlantic—eight cold, drizzly sunless days in a second-rate Cunarder. Grey walls, chipped and broken where plaster had at last fallen before autumnal rainstorms and the bitter frost of Canadian winters. It was raining. Large crates, machinery and the baggage of some unlucky passenger stood abandoned among the puddles on the wharf. The splash of harbour water in the narrow gulf between the liner's hull and the jetty syncopated the heavy beat of rain on the roof. For the first time since I had decided to leave London and try my luck in the new world my courage faltered. What hope could I have of succeeding in a place like this?"[1]

When he arrived, he knew not a soul in Canada except a kindly Toronto jazz musician who arranged to rent him a $10-per-month room in a basement. On one of his first nights ashore, Ondaatje took his guitar to an impromptu gig in a derelict jazz cellar. "I let the notes and the beats

1. This passage is taken from *Fool's Gold*, Christopher Ondaatje's only novel, published under the pseudonym Simon Marawille. More cathartic than literary, it did reveal the author's ability to capture the nuances of human frailty, including his own. The author's true identity was not difficult to establish, since the central character of his tale of financial intrigue was described as "a Canadian immigrant on the make from landed Dutch stock in faraway Ceylon . . . the disinherited hero fighting to recover lost grandeur."

carry my mind to another place," he reminisced. "My eyes closed, I began to imagine the soaring flight of my own improvisation and longed to be coaxing it from my guitar at that moment. That was how I felt now. A non-musician could never really know what it was like to be part of that sound, to actually *make* the notes yourself. It was something I could never describe to anyone else—not even another jazz musician—because the language just didn't have words for it, because the experiences were limited to so few people . . ."

Within three years of his arrival he married "the only person who understood the devils in me", Latvian-born Valda Bulins, a serene beauty with a cool intellect who lovingly sustained him through many crises. They have three grown children: David, Sarah and Jans. Nine years after his North American musical debut, spent mostly apprenticing to the financial sector in minor but instructive positions, Ondaatje got lucky. He joined a group of young sportsmen determined to regain the country's once undisputed mastery of the Olympic high-risk sport of bobsledding. His 4-man sled came in 14th (out of 26 competitors) while his team mates' sled won the Gold Medal at the 1964 Olympic Games at Innsbruck, Austria. Being part of that blithe romp made him the envy of youthful jocks in the business world, and gave him an entrée to doors then closed to immigrants.

Whatever recognition he gained was incidental in his quest to validate his still fragile sense of self and his hopes of belonging. He was eventually welcomed to graze on the business establishment's pastures, because they could not deny his energy and his intuitive wisdom. But he often felt himself to be a barely tolerated visitor. We refugees, no matter how much we pretend otherwise, seem permanently infected with the germ of distance.

Ondaatje was tolerated and even celebrated for the very good reason that he was very good at what he did, and remained so fiercely focused that few could argue with his positions. "Paper and finance, not production processes and workers, were what really interested me," he recalled. The confident forecast of the past thirty years predicting the paperless society never came to pass, which is why this book remains so relevant. Christopher's formula for success ultimately winnowed down to two personal commandments: "You never go broke taking profits." And, as his competitors learned to their sorrow, "All I want is an unfair advantage."

As this book documents, Ondaatje incorporated his main growth engine as a tiny publishing house, on 17 April 1967, with an original investment of $3,000. Within the following decade, the Pagurian Corporation became the largest publisher of art and outdoor books in the country (and if Canada has anything, it has a lot of outdoors). It exported more volumes to the United States than any of its competitors and eventually netted a tidy profit of $660,000. Typically, the firm's best seller was a book on Canadian Prime Ministers written by its president and controlling shareholder, which eventually sold 600,000 copies. True to its name ('pagurians' are hermit crabs that make their homes in larger molluscs' shells) the company's books were distributed by larger houses, a tactic that saved considerable overhead. Pagurian eventually turned itself into an immensely profitable investment trust. The firm's mission statement was simplicity itself. It called for the doubling of assets and after-tax profits each year. For a considerable time, Ondaatje actually managed to deliver that unlikely bonanza, even though for most of its existence the company employed a staff of only four or fewer people. By the time two establishment figures, Richard Bonnycastle and Donald C. Webster, joined its board in 1981, Pagurian was comfortably ensconced in a heritage house on Toronto's trendy Hazelton Avenue, which combined its corporate headquarters with an art gallery—both busy profit centres. The company actually made serious money on Canadian paintings, specializing in the extroverted canvases of William Kurelek, a Ukrainian immigrant who brought to painting the same sense of wonder as Ondaatje felt about his new home country.

At the same time, along with two partners Charles B. "Chuck" Loewen (the organizational genius) and Frederick C. McCutcheon (who had the contacts) Ondaatje disturbed Bay Street's sleepy lagoon by establishing its first major institutional brokerage firm. It wrote its own rules and quickly became the Street's most profitable shop. "It was a splendid adventure," recalled Trevor Wilson, one of the firm's senior executives, "and it was Christopher who gave the firm the nerve and the edge that we needed."

Ondaatje's most publicized declaration of independence was choosing Pierre Trudeau as the recipient of the annual Pagurian Award for Excellence. Most of Bay Street's heavy hitters had treated that luminous politician as a Communist lackey and spent millions to ensure his defeat. Yet they dared not refuse Ondaatje's invitation to the ceremony that saluted the former PM's "statesmanship". Realizing he was in hostile territory, Trudeau replied to Ondaatje's grandiloquent toast with one word: "Thanks." The throng of money men gave the ex-PM a standing ovation, while the Ceylonese immigrant beamed his approval.

His company broke most of Bay Street's rules of corporate etiquette. Diana Ross turned up late and disturbed the opening of an annual meeting and a Pagurian-sponsored Mt. Everest climber (who had carried the firm's annual report to its peak) gave a slide presentation of his successful climb. One noon hour, in the summer of 1983, Prince Andrew dropped in to visit Christopher over an intimate little lunch, and held up traffic on King Street.

By 1988 the firm's net worth had climbed to $500 million, controlling assets of $1.2 billion, and that seemed like a good moment for Ondaatje to move on. He had gone off to Tanzania for four weeks into the Serengeti preserve to reconsider his future: "Immediately my head cleared," he recalled. "You go 7,000 miles away and you see people herding cattle and looking for water to survive. It absolutely shattered me. I had been a slave to the world of finance for 40 years. It was time to get back to my true love, writing and publishing." One evening he lay motionless while a hungry lioness pawed the tent flaps at his secluded campsite. She was so close he could smell her wet fur. The journey also reawakened his affinity for leopards. "I had this love affair by identifying with it, and a love affair by searching for it. What was it I was looking for? Had I lost my way? Why was I rumbling 800 miles across the Serengeti just to search for a leopard that might not even be there?" he wrote. Most important, the visit allowed him to slow down, especially when he was taking photographs. He discovered that you cannot rush the perfect shot of a lion yawning. It took him three hours under the bone-bleaching sun to capture a giraffe with an erection.

Within eight days after his return to Canada, he decided to move permanently to England, and be English. He sold the position in his brokerage house for "many millions" and shortly afterwards gave up control of Pagurian in a share swap with the Edper Bronfmans that at the time was worth "more money than I had ever dreamed of." Pagurian shareholders lost their independence by being absorbed into what eventually became Brookfield Asset Management, but the value of their stock eventually increased from $8.50 to $50.00.

"I had heard so many stories about Ondaatje," recalled one investment analyst who attended one of his final receptions, "that when I shook hands with him I didn't know whether to count my fingers or ask for an autograph." Chances are he was too shy to do either, though he should have done both. Canadians specialize in being deferential and pretending that they live in a classless society, belonging to what George Orwell humorously called "the lower-upper-middle class".

Orwell's wise comment certainly applied to Canada's social structure. Even if he grew to love the large land which he called home for most of his life and became one of its most generous benefactors, Ondaatje never really fitted into the egalitarian imperatives of its northern latitudes. His pedigree preceded his entitlements. Born into the inbred elite of pre-independence Ceylon, his dynasty had enjoyed three centuries of tenured tea and rubber plantations, mansions and the conspicuous consumption of the leisured gentry. Family members spoke with the exaggerated upper class honk of the colonial aristocracy.

"Chris wears his inheritance like a shroud," wrote David Olive, the most perceptive of Canadian business journalists. "When he looks back, he is not able to revel in the joyous absurdity of it all: his mother, Doris, spending each August, all of August, at the races; the father, Mervyn, his courage fired by gin and invoking the authority of his membership in the Ceylon Light Infantry, hijacking trains at gunpoint and demanding the passengers join him in impromptu six-hour parties on the Trinco-Colombo run. At one point, he brought an entire public procession to a halt by throwing himself, in an alcoholic frenzy, in front of the lead elephant. Mostly what Chris feels is pain, the sense of having made an unwilling sacrifice in being torn away from the land of the Kandyan kings, with whom his father had encouraged him to feel a kinship during their long walks in the Sinhalese ruins. He was the eldest child, meant to inherit the fortune his grandfather had accumulated through astute real estate transactions. When he learned in his late teens that the money had run out and that his parents had separated, he vowed that he would recapture the lost fortune and the lost honour that had belonged to the scores of distinguished judges, politicians and tycoons who had carried the Ondaatje name through 350 years of Ceylonese history before it all ended with the colony's independence in 1948."

That betrayal still rankles: "Twisted and maddened with alcohol, my father had become another person, coarse, cruel, and driven by inexplicable rages. I was not going to be like him. I was going to be richer and stronger and better. Perhaps it was in my mind to redeem his imperfections in my own life. That could have been the reason why I was driven by a restless ambition to succeed." Having become that introspective, he turned confessional: "I had a corresponding tendency to self-deceit. I thought I wanted money so I could make it as a Canadian, telling myself it was the culture of my new country, not I, that laid so heavy a stress on material success. I conned myself into believing I merely wanted to abide by the great Canadian ethic: the religion of Mammon. I actually convinced myself that I was becoming a good Canadian. I was not a financer. I am a student of finance. And I didn't choose money. I chose to be wealthy. It's very different. I chose money because I wanted to re-establish my family, because of things I wanted to do with it. I've given most of my money away now anyway. You cannot rule from the grave. All you can do is try to do the best while you're alive."

Despite every outward sign that he is one of those rare humans who has met and exceeded his dreams, there remains a sense of poignancy in the man, as if he was still seeking the path of his lodestar. His protective colouration to all but his intimates has been the appearance he exuded of feeling uninvolved and uncaring. Seldom did he give himself away, substituting dashes of hauteur for compassion. Rhetoric for emotion. It was a false front. His problem was that he cared too much. He had within him that intensity of feeling that allows masters of the stage to hold their audiences in thrall. They know that great performances are cumulative, built from one moment to the next. "You shouldn't even try to explain this mystery inside you," declared the French film star, Simone Signoret. "You either have it, or you haven't." Ondaatje has it in spades.

As I turned the final pages of *The Power of Paper* my impulse was to read it over again, since one sitting can't do it justice. And neither can my superficial canter through Christopher Ondaatje's journey. All that can be said in certitude is that his path will take several more detours, and lead him to several more books that at the moment he has no intention of writing. "Valda and I continue to discuss and think about the next stage of our lives. England has been great but I don't think either of us wants to die here," he wrote me in a recent letter. Rocking chairs on porches were not built for this man.

Lives are viewed mostly in retrospect, as Samuel Taylor Coleridge noted so long ago, when he wrote: "The stern light of a ship illuminates only the track it has already passed." And that has been true of this book's author: every experience led him to another, so that the angle of each bounce determined the direction of his life. The ball is still bouncing . . .

PETER C. NEWMAN

26

# CHAPTER 1

## *Riches from Rags: The Uses of Paper*

*What would a world without paper be like? . . . No newspaper to read at breakfast, an unfiltered coffee, no kitchen tissues to wipe the table, no cigarettes after dinner, no bank notes to pay for a subway ticket (which wouldn't exist anyway), no letters or faxes in the office, no paper to print out emails, no paper to write on, no envelopes and no stamps, no photos of loved ones, no paper napkins for lunch, no magazines to read during breaks, no paper bags for carrying the shopping, no boxes to protect important goods, no book to read in bed.*

CONFEDERATION OF EUROPEAN PAPER INDUSTRIES

As a young boy growing up in the 1930s on a Ceylon tea plantation, I never played with toys. My chief interest was in wildlife, especially birds, and adventure. I used to collect birds' eggs, even though collecting was forbidden at my boarding school. When I was nine or ten, a boy showed me a paperback guide to the birds of Ceylon with many illustrations and detailed descriptions. He was willing to sell me the book, but I didn't have the money. Since I badly wanted it, I decided to write a letter to my father. My father knew I was interested in birds, and my parents were always complaining that I didn't write to them from school. Had I simply telephoned home, I knew the odds on success were much lower. So I took real trouble over this letter. It was neat, plaintive and carefully constructed—and it got me the money. My father replied with the requested rupees and a nice note signed "Love Daddy".

Of course I thanked him profusely, butI remember being astounded by the effect that a single sheet of paper could have. Without thinking of it, I had conducted my very first paper trade: in exchange for a letter, something my parents wanted, I had received some paper currency, which I wanted.

But with the benefit of hindsight, I can see there is much more contained in this trivial childhood memory than money. Besides the seed of my fascination with paper, it also contains the beginnings of my lifelong love of writing, books and art. At public school in England in my teens, I longed to be accepted as a writer—to be published in the school magazine, to win an essay prize. I even cherished hopes of working for the highbrow Third Programme on BBC Radio. Nothing came of any of this. The best I could manage was a distinction in the divinity paper of an exam, before I had to leave the school prematurely. My parents simply did not have the money to pay the school fees.

Some years later, in my early twenties, while drudging in a London bank, I went to a lecture at the London School of Economics and had an epiphany about paper and its dominance in the world. Suddenly I saw the power of loans, bonds, shares, bills of exchange and other financial instruments—words on paper with monetary value.

Fuelled with excitement and ambition, in 1956 I emigrated to Canada and became embroiled in corporate finance: the use of paper to create new companies. In 1967, I founded a book publishing company, Pagurian Press, and in 1970, along with two other Canadians I started a brokerage company dealing in paper investments. In the 1970s, Pagurian began to publish fine-art books and reproductions by commissioning new work from North American artists, including a noted wildlife artist; and we established a private gallery in Toronto as an outlet for the art. During the 1980s, all my interests in paper—financial instruments, books and fine art—converged in one company, the Pagurian Corporation, which expanded beyond my wildest dreams into a sprawling empire of paper. Eventually, disgusted with the greed of the North American financial scene, I decided that it was time to get out, and in 1988 I sold up, abandoned the world of high finance and returned to my teenage passions: adventure, books, art, photography and writing. Someone in the literary world might say I had been poisoning myself. And it was true: I had sold my soul to the devil because I wanted to make money. But my heart had always been in the literary world.

Nevertheless, even though I am no longer active in corporate finance, I remain deeply interested in the power of paper—how it arises and how it is best put to work. The incredible influence paper has exerted on my life has inspired a curiosity in me about the history of paper. This book is about how paper came into being, how it was used in the past, and how it is being used today—and perhaps abused. While the book is by no means intended as an autobiography, I have used my own experience in certain places, notably in chapter five, in order to dramatize the book's main theme of the power of paper.

*    *    *

Paper is attested as a word in English from the fourteenth century, the time of Geoffrey Chaucer. It derives from the Latin *papyrus*, the word used by the Romans for the paper-like material made from the papyrus plant that had been the medium for manuscripts in ancient Egypt from the end of the fourth millennium BC. (The oldest known papyrus roll, which is uninscribed, found in a tomb at Saqqara near Cairo, dates from 3035 BC.) But although papyrus has an arguable claim to be the world's first paper, in modern usage a distinction is normally drawn between papyrus and paper. 'Paper' generally refers not to the older papyrus but to the younger material made from cellulose fibres first produced in China about two millennia ago.

Before papyrus and paper, diverse materials were used for communication and administration. In the Ice Age, cave walls were painted with mysterious signs and images, as in the astonishing paintings of Lascaux. The Chauvet cave paintings, discovered in France in 1994, are

*Loan contract written in Greek, ink on papyrus from Egypt,* AD 252.
*Paper is attested as a word in English from the fourteenth century derived from
the Latin* papyrus, *the word used by the Romans for the paper-like material
made from the papyrus plant.*

approximately 31,000 years old, while those in the Fumane cave in Italy, discovered in 2000, are thought to be between 32,000 and 36,500 years old. Somewhat later than this, dated to around 13,500 BC, are the engraved and notched eagle bones also found in France; the patterns on the bones may be a lunar notation, a kind of prehistoric calendar. In the Middle East, from about 8000 BC, clay 'tokens' of varying shape, some of them inscribed with simple marks, seem to have been used for accounting and trading purposes. Around 4000 BC, in Southeast Asia, and later elsewhere in Asia, *tapa*, a material derived from the bark of the mulberry tree, was used as a proto-paper; it was a versatile substance also suitable for making clothing and bedding. Other materials, such as bamboo, linen, palm leaves, parchment, rice, silk, slate, wax and wood were also used, both before and after the invention of paper in China. As Lilian Bell describes in *Papyrus, Tapa, Amate and Rice Paper: Papermaking in Africa, the Pacific, Latin America and Southeast Asia*, the Maya, Zapotec, Mixtec and Aztec civilizations of Central America had their own 'paper'—*amate* (a Spanish word derived from an Aztec word). *Amate* was made from the bark of fig trees and it allowed the creation of books, writes Bell,

> which included a large literature on religion and rituals, books about statistics, accounts and fiscal documents, astronomy, geography and maps, records of current and historical events, wars and customs like the calendar, festivities, dreams, omens and prophecy, baptism and rites and ceremonies relating to marriage. The historical documents were often used as a legal basis for claims to land and allowances.

Painting makes paper valuable, but writing makes it powerful. The earliest writing appeared at about the same time as papyrus. It is not clear whether writing was invented first in Egypt or in neighbouring Mesopotamia—or whether the invention was simultaneous in both places, independently of each other. Currently, the oldest known written

*The oldest known written documents are clay tablets found at Warka in Southern Iraq dating from c.3300 BC*

documents in the world are clay tablets found at Warka, ancient Uruk (biblical Erech) in southern Iraq, which have been dated to about 3300 BC. They appear to have come into existence in response to an expanding economy among the Sumerian people of the area. In other words, trade and administration had become too complex to be held in the memory of the Sumerian governing elite. A reliable, permanent form of recording was required, to record, for example, the distribution of grain rations to labourers and craftsmen. "Administrators and merchants could then say the Sumerian equivalents of 'I shall put it in writing' and 'Can I have this in writing?'," writes Andrew Robinson in *The Story of Writing: Alphabets, Hieroglyphs and Pictograms*. "Writing was devised, purely and simply, as a solution to an account/technical problem, not for the perpetuation of myths, epics, hymns, historical records, or royal propaganda," notes D. T. Potts in his article, "Before Alexandria: libraries in the Ancient Near East".

But while this was true of Mesopotamia, with other cultures the earliest surviving writing is by no means always commercial. In Egypt,

*Opposite and right: account rations tablet issued to male and female workers, Ur III period, dating from the twenty-first century BC. The cuneiform inscription was written on clay and then fired, hence its survival over four millenia.*

the oldest hieroglyphic writing does indeed concern myths, historical records and royal propaganda; in China, the earliest Chinese character writing, the so-called oracle-bone inscriptions dated to 1200 BC, concern prognostication about the future; in Mexico, the earliest fully fledged New World writing, the Mayan hieroglyphs, dating from the third century AD, is concerned with religion and historical records. None of the early Greek alphabetic inscriptions—the oldest, dating to about 730 BC, is on a vase from Athens that seems to have been a prize for dancing—refers to commercial transactions. On the other hand, it may be that in all these cultures, commercial accounts existed in reality from the beginning but, unlike in Warka, such transient records did not survive the ravages of time. The reason that we still have the famous, if physically unimpressive, Linear B accounting tablets of the Minoans found in Knossos in Crete—the earliest readable European writing dating from the period 1450–1200 BC, before the Trojan War—is that a fire destroyed the palace at Knossos, baking the clay and preserving the tablets for archaeologists to excavate in the twentieth century AD.

33

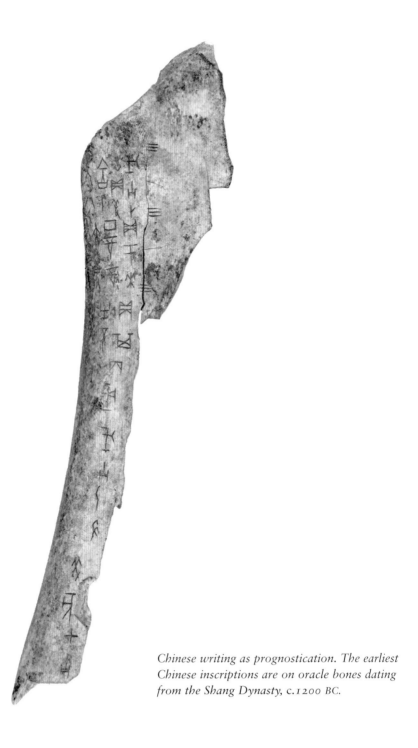

*Chinese writing as prognostication. The earliest Chinese inscriptions are on oracle bones dating from the Shang Dynasty, c.1200 BC.*

*The earliest Greek
inscription on a vase
from Athens, dating
from c.730 BC*

Whether we regard papyrus as paper or not, its connection with paper is a very close one, and its importance in the development of western civilization makes it well worth discussing.

Papyrus was made from the inner pith of the triangular stem of tall papyrus plants growing beside the River Nile. Flat strips of pith were soaked in water until they were pliable, then laid side by side and over-lapped in layers at right angles to each other. When the layers were then pressed together using hammers and weights, the gluey sap ensured adhesion; once dry, they became strong and flexible sheets.

Papyrus was a suitable writing material for several reasons. Its surface was relatively non-absorbent, so that the clarity of inscriptions on papyrus was excellent and corrections could be made by wiping the papyrus with a damp rag. (The converse was that it lent itself easily to forgery.) Moreover, the flexibility of papyrus meant that it could be rolled, a fact which enabled the ancient Egyptians to produce manuscripts varying in size from small sheets to rolls as long as 75 feet. Probably the most famous papyrus is the Book of the Dead, a funerary text first introduced into burials around 1600 BC and subsequently reproduced in multiple versions. Known to the Egyptians as the "spell for coming forth by day", the Book of the Dead contained about 200 spells and invocations intended to protect the deceased as he or she passed through various stages of the underworld.

The finest-quality papyrus sheets were almost white in colour and belonged to the first part of the second millennium, the Middle Kingdom of Pharaonic rule, while the worst were brown and coarse and were produced in the Greek and later periods from the third century BC onwards. By 600 BC, papyrus began to be exported to other countries, including Greece, and by 30 BC, when the Romans took Egypt from the

*The first Egyptian Book of the Dead dates from the 16th century BC. This illustration, dating from c.1250 BC, is from chapter 185 (Adoration of Osiris) showing the four riders of Heaven and the four triads of Gods, and Ani and his wife before a table of offerings.*

Ptolemies, papyrus had became the preferred writing material for the entire Mediterranean area. Not until the fourth century AD did parchment and vellum (a fine parchment made from the skin of a calf) supersede papyrus as the best writing material for books. Though costly to produce, parchment and vellum were more durable than papyrus, and allowed writing on both sides. (The finest papyrus manuscripts are generally, though not exclusively, written on one side only.)

The ubiquity and influence of papyrus was presumably a significant factor in Alexander the Great's reported wish to have a major library built in the new city of Alexandria, dedicated to the Muses. According to a later, if somewhat doubtful, source, the library was commissioned after Alexander's death in 323 BC by one of his generals, Ptolemy I Soter, who ruled Egypt from 305–285. Clearly Alexander's learned upbringing, as Aristotle's most famous pupil, must have been important in his decision,

*Ptolemy II Philadelphus (309–246 BC) presided over the production of perhaps the most notable book in the library of Alexandria, the translation of the first five books of the Bible into Greek.*

too; and he would also have had strategic reasons for creating a library, suggests Roy MacLeod, editor of *The Library of Alexandria*: "It was an axiom of Alexander that in order to govern, conquerors must first know whom they govern. By extension, this required the collection and translation of local literatures into Greek." He was preceded in his view by others such as Peisistratus, the tyrant of Athens in the sixth century BC, who was the first Greek to found a library, which was subsequently taken by Xerxes to Persia—"an act which set a fashion for sovereigns and sovereign cities, to seek out the books of all peoples, especially those of alien and conquered lands; and by the act of translating, render them, their languages, and their peoples members of the dominant culture," writes MacLeod. Libraries full of papyrus manuscripts (or alternatively clay tablets in Mesopotamia) became an accepted way of demonstrating the power of civilizations.

The Alexandria library differed from other ancient libraries, however,

*A curved granite wall engraved with lettering from all the world's languages surrounds part of the new Bibliotheca Alexandrina Library opened in 2001.*

in that it aimed to include everything ever written. Excavations of several royal libraries in Mesopotamia, in particular that of Ashurbanipal, the seventh-century ruler of Assyria, have shown that they were national rather than international libraries. Perhaps the most notable book in the Alexandria library was part of the Bible—the first five books known as the Pentateuch—translated from Hebrew into Greek in 281 BC in the time of Ptolemy II Philadelphus, probably by 71 scholars. The purpose was not so much pious as to attract Hebrew and Greek scholars to the library in Alexandria. Nina Collins, in *The Library in Alexandria and the Bible in Greek*, sees the project as an event with far-reaching consequences: "This brought about the wide distribution of written, Jewish scriptures into the non-Jewish world, which in turn lead to the birth of Christianity and the western civilization that we know today." Thus did Alexandria became a centre for learning, incorporating Babylonian, Egyptian, Jewish and Greek thought. Robert Barnes remarks in *The Library of Alexandria*: "It is noteworthy that the Athenian democracy (and for that matter the Roman Republic) never created a public library. It was only the cultural pretensions of tyrants, kings and emperors which could conceive anything like a universal collection of books."

Much confusion surrounds the final fate of the great library. It is said that a fire destroyed it in 48 BC during fighting between Julius Caesar and Cleopatra or Ptolemy XIII for control of Alexandria. Another story blames some of the destruction on Christian fanaticism in the late fourth century AD. Yet another story blames it on the Islamic fanaticism of the Arabs, who conquered Alexandria in AD 642 and are said to have burned the library deliberately because it was a pagan collection. While there is solid evidence for the first story, the destruction was certainly not complete in 48 BC, and there are references by Roman writers to the continuing existence of the library as late as 272. In 391, attempts to Christianize the city by the patriarch of Alexandria, Theophilus, led to street fighting, much destruction and the departure from the city of scholars and philosophers—presumably carrying whatever manuscripts they could salvage. There is no credible evidence at all for the Arab destruction of the library. What seems most likely is that the library of Alexandria was destroyed or dispersed by the end of the fourth century AD, six or seven centuries after its founding by Ptolemy I.

For the next millennium and a half, the library retreated largely into the realm of myth and legend, as a lost wonder of the ancient world. No one even knew exactly where it had once stood. When, in 1974, during an American presidential visit to Alexandria, Richard Nixon innocently enquired about the library's location before its destruction by fire, there was an embarrassed silence from his hosts. The Egyptian government ordered an investigation, and eventually this became the foundation for a revival of the library. A striking new building was commissioned in 1990 after the Aswan declaration, with funding from the Egyptian government and Unesco, and opened in 2001 to greet both a new millennium and the new age of electronic information. The Bibliotheca Alexandrina, intended as both a library and a conference centre, shows the continuing power of paper over the human imagination.

The invention of paper in China may go as far back as the sixth or fifth century BC, when the washing of hemp and linen rags is attested—someone could have stumbled on the possibility while drying some wet refuse fibres on a mat. Certainly, very early specimens of paper preserved by arid conditions at sites in western China suggest that paper-making probably began in the tropical regions of south and southeast China in the second century BC. The traditional date for its invention, however, is AD 105. In that year, the Emperor Ho Ti was presented with a sample of *zhi* by Ts'ai Lun (Cai Lun), a court official, *zhi* being a substance defined by a contemporary dictionary as being a mat of refuse fibres, made out of macerated tree bark, the remnants of hemp, rags of cloth and old fishing nets. It appears that Ts'ai Lun had found a new treatment that improved on existing types of paper, perhaps by reducing its surface absorbency. At any rate, his *zhi* provided a more usable, and much cheaper, writing surface than the pure silk used by the court.

Ts'ai Lun was a eunuch who entered the imperial service in AD 75, was soon appointed political adviser to Emperor Ho Ti, and eventually became chief eunuch. Among his varied duties were the making of swords and furniture for the imperial household, and the preservation of thousands of bamboo books as the head of the Imperial Study Department. This latter laborious task is said to have led Ts'ai Lun to seek a lighter, alternative material for books—paper. His luck continued under the successor regime of the Dowager Empress T'eng, who acted as regent for a child emperor, and Ts'ai Lun was ennobled, but when his patron died from overwork at the age of only 41, political opponents of the Dowager spread rumours that her family was plotting to overthrow the Emperor. Because of Ts'ai Lun's close affiliation with the family, he was implicated, though falsely. The story goes, that he received an imperial summons which meant certain execution. Instead of attending court, he returned to his house. After bathing and dressing in his finest robes, he committed suicide by drinking wine mixed with a drug he had always carried on his person since the death of his patron, carefully wrapped in some paper he had manufactured while he was chief of the Imperial Supply Department.

By the second century AD, paper and paper-making were widespread in much of China. Then they spread to Korea and Japan and western China. In about 770, the Japanese Empress Shotoku commissioned a million paper prayers, block printed by hand, to mark the end of an eight-year civil war, each of which was to be rolled up and inserted into a tiny pagoda; the task required 157 men to work for six years. On the Silk Road through Central Asia, the widespread Chinese use of paper in business has been confirmed by the discovery of documents in Turfan, in western China. Excavated tombs have revealed people buried in hats, shoes and belts made from recycled paper, and even a papier mâché coffin made from government documents dating from 769, the year the official died. Such documents—the ones from the coffin all concerned the provisioning of long-distance horses used by government officials—have given researchers an unexpectedly detailed picture of commercial life on the Silk Road during the Tang dynasty (AD 618–907).

However, for most of this early period, Ts'ai Lun's revolutionary invention was confined to China, Korea and Japan. Although Ts'ai Lun is well known in the Far East as the inventor of paper, in the West his name is hardly known. He surely deserves to be as familiar a name as Johannes Gutenberg, the inventor of moveable type, even if Ts'ai Lun did take an already existing substance and re-invent it. The reason he is not, is probably because paper took over a millennium to catch on in Europe and did not reach the West directly from China but came via the Muslim world, as we shall shortly see.

But first let us consider the Chinese invention of paper money. The earliest recorded use of paper as money dates from the late tenth century, but at this time the notes were more like banker's drafts than our present-day concept of fully negotiable banknotes. However the concept fairly quickly evolved to the point where 16 merchant houses issued notes for the Chinese government, backed by cash reserves. In the words of Richard Goetzmann and Geert Rouwenhorst, editors of *The Origins of Value: The Financial Innovations That Created Modern Capital Markets*, "true negotiability first developed in China and reached its most dramatic expression in the eleventh century in the form of paper money. Indeed, the Chinese not only invented paper money, they invented fiat money—that is, cash that is negotiable just because the government says so."

Richard von Glahn, in the same book, has traced the fascinating origins of paper money in detail. In 960, the Song dynasty was founded and the Chinese Empire was reunified. As a result, trade flourished, and there was a shortage of coins. In contrast with European coins, Chinese coins were made of low-value metals like copper and iron because these were easier for the Emperor to control. But iron coins were burdensome to transport. A housewife had to bring a pound and a half of iron coins to market simply to buy a pound of salt. Iron currency became devalued, especially in Sichuan province, where trade was the most buoyant as a

42

result of the province's abundance of silk and tea. A rebellion in 993, partly in response to the shortage and inconvenience of iron currency, resulted in the closing of iron mints. Merchants were prompted to issue their own paper notes, which began to function as currency. These notes were most probably exchangeable for cash deposits, silk, or gold and silver.

Such privately backed notes allowed trade to continue, but a succession of court cases showed that the notes were being abused, and so the imperial government intervened. It reopened the iron mints and decreed that only certain merchant houses could issue notes. Still the system was not tightly enough regulated: the merchants issuing the bills often used the cash deposits they received to buy property, creating a problem with liquidity. Eventually, only government-run houses were permitted to issue notes. The notes were valid for a maximum of two years to prevent excess wear and counterfeiting, and to control the amount of notes in circulation. Now the money supply was once again firmly in the hands of the Emperor, but in the form of paper as well as metal. Von Glahn comments:

> In contrast to western monetary thought, which addressed the problem of determining a just price for commodities exchanged in market transactions, Chinese monetary thought and policy was predicated on enabling the ruler to overcome the vicissitudes of dearth and plenty and to provide for the material needs of his subjects. The ruler could accomplish this goal by tightly controlling the supply of money to ensure stable prices and ample supplies of goods . . . It is the ruler's stamp, not the intrinsic values of the monetary medium, that confers value.

The system worked, until the Song government made the mistake of printing excess notes in an attempt to alleviate a financial crisis. The value of the notes fell and inflation soared. But eventually the government established a viable fiat currency. By the end of the Northern Song period in 1127, paper money was in wide circulation—in China, if in no other country.

Given the Chinese use of paper on the Silk Road, it was inevitable that paper would spread across Asia. The process was well underway by the eighth century through the conduit of Islamic civilization in Central Asia and the Middle East. It was the Muslims who introduced paper to India, though not until about the eleventh century—surprisingly late, given the ancient Indian tradition of writing on talipot palm leaves. (One reason may have been that paper quickly deteriorates in a monsoon climate with humidity and insect attacks; another possibility is that high-caste Indians feared pollution from a substance made from rags.) Around the same time, the Muslims also introduced paper to Europe.

As with Ts'ai Lun's invention of paper, there is a traditional date for the encounter between paper and Islam. In 751, there was a battle at Talas—a city in southern Kazakhstan where the Silk Road crosses the Talas River—between the eastward-expanding forces of the newly established Abbasid caliphate, based in Baghdad, and those of the westward-expanding Chinese Empire. The Arab commander Ziyad ibn Salih was victorious, the Tang dynasty's westward advance was halted, and the various silk routes were opened up to the Arabs. A lesser consequence was that Chinese paper-makers captured in the battle were taken to Samarkand, in Uzbekistan, where they were said to have founded the Arab paper industry.

Jonathan Bloom, in *Paper Before Print: The History and Impact of Paper in the Islamic World*, is sceptical about the importance of this event. The battle of Talas was not pivotal in the story of paper, says Bloom, because archaeological evidence suggests that paper-making was already being practiced throughout Central Asia by 751, including in Samarkand. For example, there are paper documents which were discovered at Mount Mugh, a mountain stronghold in Tajikistan, dating from the period 722–23, when the ruler of Samarkand took refuge on the mountain from Arab invaders. Bloom regards the tale of the Chinese paper-makers captured in 751 as being as likely as the story of Ts'ai Lun's single-handed invention of paper in 105. According to him:

> The story of Cai [Ts'ai] Lun is a pleasant fiction made up long after the events in question to add colour to a long and obscure process . . . Much as Cai Lun's invention of paper remains a convenient metaphor for the underlying truth that paper began to be used for writing in early second-century China, the story of captured Chinese paper-makers metaphorically describes how paper was introduced to the Islamic lands through Central Asia at a time when, under Abbasid rule, this region began to play an increasingly important role in Islamic civilization.

Whether we accept the tradition or not, what is indisputable is that in the eighth century Samarkand became a vital centre of paper production, from which paper-making spread to the Middle East. The first paper mill in Baghdad was established in 794–95, and it produced enough paper to replace papyrus in accounts and administration. Indeed bureaucrats preferred paper to papyrus, because written entries on paper were more permanent and less forgeable. The oldest complete book in Arabic is dated 848. By the middle of the ninth century—barely a century since Muslims had first encountered paper—many, if not most, lettered Muslims, as well as Christians and Jews, were using it for writing letters, keeping records, and copying literary and theological works, notes Bloom. For a while Baghdad, the capital of the Abbasid caliphs, remained the centre for paper-making in the Muslim world, then the craft spread to Syria (Damascus) and Egypt (Cairo), where it took strong root. In Damascus, daily paper-based despatches carried by pigeons helped the ruler to keep tabs on outlying regions. In Cairo, the paper-makers produced a coarse wrapping paper for grocers, rumoured to be made from hempen winding-sheets stolen from tombs by grave-robbers. The versatility of paper ensured its rapid growth.

The Abbasid caliphate, which ruled from 750–1258, brought about a golden age for the arts and learning, in which paper played a vital role. Of course much of the learning was religious, for which paper was not deemed to be a fit medium until as late as 1000 (until then religious texts were written on parchment). Still other learning was government inspired, and produced legal and administrative texts. However, sheer curiosity and respect for knowledge also drove Abbasid authors to write works on philosophy, geography and navigation, mathematics and applied science, astronomy, astrology, medicine and alchemy. As for imaginative literature, there was "a veritable explosion", writes Bloom, in the writing and compiling of Arabic poetry, stories and other works of fiction—epitomized by the stories about the court of the fifth Caliph, Harun ar-Rashid, collected in *The Arabian Nights*. Paper facilitated all such intellectual and artistic activities. In architecture and decoration, tiling and carpet patterns could be designed in advance on paper. Music, genealogical trees and maps could all be conveniently noted down on paper. There was a spurt in making illustrated books. Cookbooks were extraordinarily popular.

As in China, paper revolutionized Islamic commerce and money. Until the arrival of paper, financial matters among the Arabs had been transacted by dactylonomy (counting on the fingers), together with the use of an abacus. Everyone was in debt and most wholesale and even retail commerce was conducted by using credit—cash was uncommon enough to warrant an immediate discount of between two and four per cent. Paper meant that agreements could be drawn up between buyers and sellers rather than coinage having to be physically transported, sometimes over long distances. Such agreements also protected against dishonesty. Financial instruments included the *suftaja*, a letter of credit which was technically a loan of money to avoid the risks of transportation, and the *sakk* or *sakka*, from which the word cheque is derived, a piece of paper which the recipient presented to a banker for payment. Promissory notes called *ruq'a*, issued by established bankers, were as good as cash and were the foundation of the Arab paper economy. As Bloom summarizes, "financial procedure in the medieval Islamic lands was complex and sophisticated, and the whole complicated edifice depended on the availability of paper. It was used for communication over long distances, for record-keeping, for transfer of cash, and for legal safeguards."

As a result of the spread of Islam, the Moorish rulers of Spain were the first to establish paper mills in Europe and introduce Christian Europe to the ancient Chinese invention. This was in the eleventh century. By the fifteenth century, most of Europe was making paper. The connection between Arabic and European paper-making can be traced directly through language. The English word ream (five hundred sheets of paper) derives from the Old French word *rayme* via the Spanish *resma*, which itself comes from the Arabic *rizmah*, meaning 'bale or bundle'.

It is interesting to speculate on what might have happened had Europeans not been introduced to paper by the Arabs and encountered it only when European travellers visited China in substantial numbers in the sixteenth century. What effect would no paper have had on the course of the European Renaissance? But in doing so, we must remember how complicated cultures really are. For example, the fact that an idea is 'in the air' does not ensure that it will be put into practice. Even though the celebrated Venetian merchant Marco Polo travelled to China in the late thirteenth century and reported to Europeans with amazement on the wonders of Chinese paper money, Europe did not actually use banknotes until four centuries after Polo's great journey.

The Moorish introduction of paper notwithstanding, Italy established a lead in European paper-making. Amalfi and Fabriano became notable centres of paper production in the thirteenth century, using improved techniques with water power and more efficient presses. Italian paper-makers were sought after in other parts of Europe. In 1390, a Nuremberg councillor, Ulmann Stromer, created his own paper mill with the help of skilled Italian workers. His diary provides evidence that his paper mill was the first in Germany, and shows that he considered paper-making to be a secret art with many technological difficulties to be surmounted.

Paper was plentiful and popular for personal use in some areas: an Italian entrepreneur, Francesco di Marco Datini of Prato, who died in 1410, left behind a staggering 140,000 letters written on paper. But the explosion in paper-making in the fourteenth century did not create a concomitant explosion in book production, because the actual process of making a book was unaltered by the availability of paper, despite its cheapness compared to parchment. When universities came into existence around this time, there was an increase in the demand for books, but books still had to be laboriously copied by scribes. The pre-printing era of European paper production is described by Elizabeth Eisenstein in *The Printing Revolution in Early Modern Europe* as follows: "Paper production served the needs of merchants, bureaucrats, preachers, and literati; it quickened the pace of correspondence and enabled more men of letters to act as their own scribes. But the same number of man-hours was still required to turn out a given text."

And now we have reached Johannes Gutenberg, the world-famous printer of Mainz. Around 1450, his moveable metal type produced the first European printed book, which in turn triggered the expansion of the empire of paper beyond anything hitherto imaginable. Gutenberg's invention of printing and the mass-production of books is undoubtedly a turning point in the history of the world. One commentator, John Man, in *The Gutenberg Revolution*, even claims: "Gutenberg's invention made the soil from which sprang modern history, science, popular literature, the emergence of the nation-state, so much of everything by which we define modernity."

Yet, as with Ts'ai Lun's paper, and many other crucial inventions, Gutenberg had predecessors. Moveable type was originally used in China in the eleventh century by Pi Sheng—at first made from baked clay, then

*Johannes Gutenberg, the world famous*
*printer of Mainz, c.1450.*

from metal (cast by pouring molten metal into sand moulds shaped with wooden blocks). Korean printers took up this technique and actually printed a 50-volume work in 1234, *Prescribed Ritual Texts of the Past and Present*. But the process was immensely labour-intensive and slow, for the simple reason that the Korean script, like the Chinese script, contained tens of thousands of signs, most of which required their own individual metal stamp. Moreover, the Koreans lacked the screw-based printing presses, common in the Middle East and Europe (where the principle had evolved for pressing olives for oil and grapes for juice in wine-making), and other metallurgical skills for cutting and casting the type that had evolved over time in Europe. Gutenberg developed a metal alloy suitable for type, a mould that could cast letters with precision, and even oil-based printing ink. In the event, Korean and Chinese printing with moveable type, though theoretically ahead of its European equivalent, made no progress because it was fundamentally impractical as compared to hand copying of manuscripts by trained calligraphers.

Finally, in defence of Gutenberg's claim to priority, it is worth saying that he invented moveable metal type wholly independently of China and Korea. Unlike paper, the knowledge of moveable type did not spread from East to West.

According to Man's study of Gutenberg, "He emerges as that rarity: a man seized by an idea, obsessed by it, *imprinted* by it, who also has the technical skill, business acumen and sheer dogged, year-after-year grit to make it real." Born in about 1400 in Mainz into a patrician family involved in coin-making, the young Johannes would have been exposed to the technical processes of making the steel punches for striking coins. Although there is no direct evidence that he acquired the skill himself, he probably acquired the expertise in metallurgy that would enable him to design metal type and become a printer. But throughout his career he lacked the financial resources to support his inventiveness. He needed a wealthy backer to invest in his big idea. In 1449, he borrowed money to buy equipment from Johann Fust, a goldsmith and merchant of Mainz, and in 1450, Gutenberg's press produced its first book, a standard Latin grammar entitled *Ars Grammatica*, 28 pages long. Its content meant that its market was guaranteed, and, being short, its production costs were low. The fact that it was printed meant that every copy was identical, and in theory error-free, unlike books copied by scribes—an advertisement of particular value for a book about grammar.

Gutenberg's most famous book is of course the Bible in Latin, printed in Mainz, probably in 1454. It is a magnificent production, made to resemble a traditional scribal Bible in regard to its margins and typeface. The paper was imported over the Alps from Italy, as its watermarks reveal, since German paper was still of inferior quality. Some 150 copies were printed on paper (of which 39 survive), and between 30 and 35 copies on vellum (of which twelve survive). It has been calculated that each copy on vellum used 170 calf skins, requiring a total of some 5–6,000 skins. To have printed all the copies on vellum would have been

*Johannes Gutenberg examines a page from his first printing press, c.1450.*

prohibitively expensive. It was the invention of moveable type *together* with the use of paper that made Gutenberg's invention both ground-breaking and commercially viable.

Gutenberg was a religious man but his main reason for choosing the Bible was that he knew it would sell to Europe's churches and rulers. To print it, however, meant that Gutenberg had to borrow more money from Fust, without having paid even the interest on the first loan. In 1455, just as the first Bible was ready, Fust sued Gutenberg for his money, arguing that he himself had borrowed the money from elsewhere and was obliged to pay interest to his creditor. After legal wrangles Fust took over Gutenberg's business in late 1455 in order to recover his money; he then became the leading printer in Mainz. Thus, on the brink of success, Gutenberg lost control of his own creation. Although he was able to continue to print, the next ten years were difficult ones for him, financially and politically, until in 1465, the Archbishop of Mainz awarded Gutenberg a pension-in-kind, with an annual measure of grain, wine, and clothing and exemption from certain taxes, in exchange for his loyalty, sworn by oath, and the services of his printing press. Gutenberg died in relative comfort in Mainz in 1468, outliving his adversary Fust, who caught the plague while on a sales trip to Paris.

For the rest of the century, books were in their infancy. (All books printed before 1501 were arbitrarily termed *incunabula*, Latin for 'swaddling clothes', by a seventeenth-century historian, and the term is still used.) It took several decades for scribal copying of books to die out altogether—along with a small, labour-intensive industry of scribes. But even before Gutenberg's death, it was obvious that printing would transform European culture.

In 1460, Gutenberg's apprentices in Mainz printed the first modern-language Bible, in German. Despite the poor quality of its translation, the Archbishop of Mainz banned it in 1485. At first the Church had favoured the printing press and used it to raise money for a crusade against the Turks after the fall of Constantinople in 1453, but as the number of printing presses grew, so did the Church's fear of their influence. By 1500, there were presses in more than 250 places in Europe and thirteen million books were circulating in a continent of 100 million people. For the first time, texts became widely available to readers who were not churchmen, and they were able to read about ideas for themselves rather than simply accept priestly authority. Printed books undoubtedly fuelled the Reformation which, led by Martin Luther after 1517, gave rise to Protestantism. "It is perhaps the case that a book on its own has never been sufficient to change anyone's mind," write Lucien Febvre and Henri-Jean Martin in *The Coming of the Book: The Impact of Printing, 1450–1800*.

> But if it does not succeed in convincing, the printed book is
> at least tangible evidence of convictions held because it

embodies and symbolizes them; it furnishes arguments to those who are already converts, lets them develop and refine their faith, offers them points which will help them to triumph in debate, and encourages the hesitant. For all these reasons books played a critical part in the development of Protestantism in the sixteenth century.

In other words, for printed books to have real influence, they require educated, curious and receptive readers. This is an important reason why printed books first appeared in Europe and why they did not immediately take hold in non-European cultures. In Russia, for example, it took another two centuries for book publishing to take root. "Printing required favourable social and cultural conditions in order to spread, and Russia's lack of a literate laity was a serious obstacle to the rise of print culture," note Asa Briggs and Peter Burke in *A Social History of the Media: From Gutenberg to the Internet*.

Other factors too come into play. Muslim cultures certainly had the social and cultural conditions conducive to the printed book, as had once been the case in Abbasid Baghdad. Briggs and Burke point out that the Turks thought it sinful to print religious books and so a fear of heresy arrested the development of a print culture. Bloom attributes its slow development to the difficulties of creating an Arabic type font, which required twice the number of pieces of type as a European font. Moreover, there was a stronger calligraphic tradition in Islamic culture compared to Europe, with which print could not easily compete.

Perhaps the most unusual of *incunabula*—and a book that would certainly never have been printed by Gutenberg—is *Hypnerotomachia Poliphili*, published in Venice in 1499. The pretentious, orotund title translates roughly as "Poliphilo's Struggle for Love in a Dream", and the author, who is coy about his identity, is thought to have been a monk in Venice who lived outside a monastery (and therefore had contact with women). Written in an artificial language with Italian grammar and words drawn from Latin, Tuscan and Greek, the book is an erotic fantasy constructed around its protagonist Poliphilo's quest to find the woman he loves. Some of the beautiful and lavish engravings would, even today, be seen as soft-core pornography, but strangely, it is architecture that gives Poliphilo (which means 'lover of many things') his keenest sexual pleasure; he also has a fetish for gardens. Although the book was a commercial disaster upon publication, within half a century it became a cult item, and today collectors will pay in the region of $750,000 for one of the hundred or so surviving copies.

The Vatican library's copy of *Hypnerotomachia Poliphili* has some of the offending parts of the illustrations inked out. As book publishing grew in maturity, so censorship of printed books went into full swing. In 1544, the Catholic Church published its first *Index of Prohibited Books*, which continued, with regular updating, down to 1966. During those four centuries the index included works by Voltaire, Flaubert, Descartes and Darwin—but not, surprisingly enough, D. H. Lawrence's *Lady Chatterley's Lover*.

Censorship by book burning also remained popular, perhaps more so in an age of mass production of books. Before print, there were notorious episodes in China, in 221 BC, when a new Emperor ordered the burning of all Confucian books, banned Confucian teaching and killed Confucian scholars; and again in Central America, after 1427, when the founder of the Aztec power burned the books of conquered peoples so that he could present his own version of history. Then, in the sixteenth century, after the Spanish conquest of Mexico, Aztec and Maya books were burned by Spaniards who regarded them as works of the devil. (Fortunately, a few survived in European libraries to aid the twentieth-century decipherment of the Mayan hieroglyphs.) In 1822, the German-Jewish poet Heinrich Heine wrote with disturbing foresight: "Where they burn books, they will, in the end, burn human beings too." Heine's books were among those incinerated in 1930s Nazi Germany by student groups, along with books by Brecht, Einstein and Freud, which were considered to be of 'un-German spirit'. At the largest book-burning bonfire in Berlin, 40,000 students gathered to hear Joseph Goebbels pronounce Jewish intellectualism dead. More recently, the publication of Salman Rushdie's *The Satanic Verses* in Britain prompted Iran's Ayatollah Khomeini to issue a *fatwa* against the author and publishers in 1989, sentencing them to death. Muslims around the world, including in Britain, protested against the novel by publicly burning it.

In England, the print revolution was defined by William Caxton, a religious man like Gutenberg. Born in Kent in 1422, Caxton was a diplomat who learnt the art of printing on the Continent—first in Cologne, then in Bruges, where he set up his first press in 1472. He used his time abroad to experiment and perfect techniques before returning to England in 1476, where he established a print shop in Westminster called the Red Pale, printing in Latin, French and English. Unlike Gutenberg, Caxton was a cautious businessman who required assurance that a proposed title would sell enough to cover its production costs. Yet Caxton too, like Gutenberg, was possessed by an idea, in his case an almost missionary zeal to improve the English language. A century before him, a contemporary of Chaucer's had described how a man from Kent and a man from London —living a mere 20 miles apart—could not understand one another. Things were hardly better in Caxton's day. In his biography of Caxton, subtitled *The First English Editor, Printer, Merchant and Translator*, Richard Deacon writes that Caxton was "a printer at war, firmly keeping his attention on the main task of propagating the English language in print. His war was against the forces of indolence, reaction, suspicion and indifference, against all who failed to realize that in the whole of Europe there was no language which was so unprogressive or crude as the conglomeration of dialects and primitive phraseology of Middle English."

However, Caxton did print Chaucer. He also introduced many new words into English, some of which are still in use. To refine English he adapted French words, since French was the accepted language of cultured people in fifteenth-century England. This is why Deacon maintains that Caxton was more important as an editor and translator than as a printer. Not only did he print works on subjects that educated Englishmen wanted to read about, the texts were in a language they could understand. Caxton's *Histories of Troy* had a direct influence on Shakespeare's *Troilus and Cressida*, and other Caxton publications influenced the poet Spenser.

Like Gutenberg, Caxton printed many religious texts, one of the earliest of which was *The Golden Legend*, published in 1484. Translated from Latin, it described miracles and the lives of the saints, with Caxton's own addition of some Bible stories. Unlike Gutenberg, though, neither Caxton nor his London contemporaries produced a modern-language Bible. Part of the reason, no doubt, was that Caxton perceived no demand for it in the English vernacular of his time, but he may also have been astute enough to realize that the Church authorities could have taken offence and finished his career as a printer. When Richard Grafton published the first English-language Bible in 1537, printed in Zurich, it met with a mixed reaction; indeed some of the edition was burned, which turned out to be good publicity for the remainder.

Caxton's press ran for fourteen years under his management with the help of three assistants. It printed nearly 80 separate books and 18,000 pages of text. Although his market was small, it did widen from court circles to include the professional classes, and his publications were certainly influential. In Deacon's analysis,

> though Caxton dealt entirely with books and pamphlets, one sees him almost as an editor of a national newspaper, shaping popular taste, taking cognizance of public opinion and deciding what kind of writing sells best. This is because in the first place the printed book was in effect the first newspaper, but much more so because Caxton wrote prologues and epilogues and edited other people's works rather as an editor appeals to mass circulations.

After Caxton died in 1491, printing continued under his former assistant, the memorably named Winkyn de Worde, who relocated the printing press from Westminster to Fleet Street in 1500 and printed 400 books over a period of 42 years.

In the first half of the sixteenth century, the Crown, as well as the Church, took up printing, aware of its power. Henry VIII of England appointed Thomas Berthelet as the King's printer in 1530, and Berthelet continued to hold this position for some 25 years. Concerned by public sympathy for his first wife, Catherine of Aragon, whom he had divorced, the King wanted to use the power of the press to improve his tyrannical public image. Berthelet's publications were designed to allay fears and prevent uprisings by suggesting that Henry took advice from wise counsellors. As Christopher Warner writes in *Henry VIII's Divorce: Literature and the Politics of the Printing Press*, Berthelet's pamphlets represented the King as "a humanistic scholar—or philosopher-king, a learned and temperate ruler who solicits the counsel of wise men assembled at his court, in the universities, and in the two houses of Parliament."

Over time, pamphlets were produced by many printers, not just on behalf of royalty. In the English Civil War, so-called 'intelligence pamphlets' were among the few ways for news to travel and influence people. Petitions also became part of the proliferation of printed paper. "The signing of petitions by a wide range of people was a practice which entered English politics in the seventeenth century. Fifteen thousand citizens of London signed the Root and Branch petition in 1640 at the beginning of the Civil War, and later petitions displayed as many as 30,000 signatures," note Briggs and Burke. Under these circumstances, the start of printed newspapers was almost inevitable. The first European newspaper was printed in Sweden in 1644; England followed 20 years later, the delay being most likely due to the upheaval of the Civil War and Cromwell's subsequent regime.

Royal censorship of the press had existed since the beginning of printing, apart from a brief period of breakdown during the Civil War, and with the launch of newspapers, it tightened. After the Restoration in England in 1660, the Licensing Act was passed, permitting only the official surveyor of the press to publish newspapers. Sir Roger L'Estrange, appointed in 1663, had a reputation for determination and severity in tracking down and punishing illegal presses, while using his position to publish official news. With the help of a businessman, L'Estrange converted the *Oxford Gazette* into a mouthpiece of officialdom, changing its name to the *London Gazette*. As England's first notable newspaper, the *London Gazette* printed all the news the court deemed fit to print and became a vital source of information for businessmen needing to know about Britain's activities overseas. It still exists, as the organ of government, mainly to publish official notices. (In 1785, a rival to the *London Gazette* appeared, *The Daily Universal Register*, which then became *The Times*.)

Communications were further improved with the printing of maps. In 1675, John Ogilby's *Britannia*, the first English road atlas, was published. But the explosion of printed matter, while it encouraged the dissemination of knowledge, also brought into question the validity of printed information (just as the growth of the internet did at the end of the twentieth century). On the one hand, knowledge of all kinds became more available and standardized because printing reproduced multiple copies; on the other hand, many erroneous facts and contradictory views jostled for attention. In 1672, the poet Marvell was moved to exclaim, "O Printing! How thou hast disturbed the peace of Mankind!"

Clearly, both governments and the governed now thought that paper and the printed word had power. As Briggs and Burke comment: "Newspapers contributed to the rise of public opinion, a term which is first recorded in French around 1750, in English in 1781."

More than newspapers and even books, banknotes encapsulate the combined power of paper and print, as mentioned earlier in relation to paper money in China. The Bank of England was established in 1694 and issued its first notes in return for deposits. To begin with, they were not printed but handwritten by the bank's cashiers for specific sums and could be redeemed for gold or coinage upon presentation of the note by the bearer. This followed the practice of goldsmith-bankers like Gutenberg's sponsor Fust, who since the sixteenth century had issued receipts known as 'running cash notes' made out to depositors of gold coins.

The Bank of England was founded for a specific purpose: to raise money for William III's war against the French. A sum of £1,200,000 was given to the bank by 1268 shareholders, and in return the bank paid eight per cent interest. In 1696, a recoinage removed the need for low-denomination notes and the lowest note issued was £50. (However, most people at this time would never have encountered such a banknote, as the average income was then only £20 per annum.) In 1725, fixed denomination notes were issued—although the £ sign and first digit were now printed, other numbers were added by hand and each note still had to be hand-signed by a cashier. By 1745, the notes ranged in denomination from £20 to £1000. It was not until the gold shortages caused by the Seven Years War that a £10 note was issued, while in 1793 the war with France provoked the issue of a £5 note. On just two occasions in its history was the Bank of England forced to stop paying out gold for its notes: during the period following the war with France, until 1819, and again during the First World War, in order for the government to preserve its stock of bullion. In 1925, the bank partially returned to the gold standard, but in 1931 it left it for good.

Only in 1855 did the Bank of England's notes become fully printed like modern banknotes. By then, there had been significant technological advances in paper-making and printing. The Fourdrinier machine, developed in France in 1799, allowed paper to be manufactured continuously. In 1843, groundwood pulp, discovered by Saxon Keller, and in 1854 chemical pulp, took over from rag-based paper. However British banknotes, like American ones, continued to be made from a special kind of paper: a combination of cotton fibre and linen rag which made them more durable than paper made from wood pulp. Improved watermarking and security printing came in too to defeat counterfeiters. By the early twentieth century, most of the basic forms of printing had been established. Photographic printing methods continued to improve and by the 1950s electronic methods were introduced. Today, printing machines can produce quality work at speeds of 10,000 sheets per hour.

Ascribing a piece of paper with a certain monetary value gives it power. When, working at a London bank in the 1950s, I suddenly grasped this fact about the capitalist system, a new world of possibility opened to me. With this knowledge, I would first deal in paper for others. Eventually I would be in a strong enough position to issue my own pieces of paper. Only then—after 20 years of hacking my way through the jungle of finance—did each bit of paper I touched seem to turn, so to speak, into gold.

# CHAPTER 2

# *Financial Instruments: The Paper Economy*

*Put a financial engineer on a desert island (or an emerging market!) and give him only a few tools, such as the means to calculate the time value of money, the ability to contract on random outcomes, and a legal structure that allows the transferability of financial claims, and most of today's financial instruments would be reconstructed.*

WILLIAM GOETZMANN AND GEERT ROUWENHORST,
*The Origins of Value, 2005*

In 1950, when I was 16, I received another life-changing letter from my parents—this time from my mother rather than my father. By now I had been sent away from Ceylon and was more or less settled at a public school in Devon. One evening, after prayers, my housemaster called me into his study and, in a voice faltering with embarrassment, broke some important news. Almost 25 years later, when the news had lost most of its power to shock me, I fictionalized the incident in a novel, *Fool's Gold*, a somewhat crudely written, semi-autobiographical story of the Canadian financial world written under a pseudonym. My central character, named Michael de Shane, spoke for me when he said of the housemaster: "At some point he gave me my mother's telegram, not that it registered right away. DADDY AND I HAVE SEPARATED PLEASE DON'T BE ANGRY ARRIVING SOUTHAMPTON SIXTEENTH DECEMBER MEET ME LOVE MOTHER. . . . I kept the news to myself, never discussed it with anyone. As a matter of fact, I was ashamed." When my mother arrived by ship in England, intending to settle in London, she told me that my father's alcoholism had finally become too much for her, and that he was heavily in debt: there was no more money to pay for my expensive English schooling.

The following year, with a bare five school certificate credits to my name, I got a job as a trainee in the National Bank of India, a Scottish bank located at 26 Bishopsgate in the City of London.

In a way, I was lucky, for I arrived at an opportune historical moment. Just three or four years before, in 1947, India had become politically independent from Britain—followed by Ceylon in 1948. The bank therefore looked favourably on me as a Ceylonese national, who could in due course be permitted to fill a post in the capital Colombo, which was an important and profitable branch of the bank. The London managers put me to work in a department dealing with shipping documents, where I learned how freight companies used bank finance to ship goods. Usually, goods were shipped and paid for on delivery, but sometimes payment was required in advance. Either way, banks were involved in the transaction—as they were, too, in underwriting insurance for the goods.

It may be hard to grasp now, decades after the end of Empire, but the fact is that right up to the late 1940s London's eastern banks, of which the National Bank of India was one of many, practically ruled the world's finance, particularly in the outposts of the British Empire. They were enormously profitable. I quickly understood this on arrival because I had been taught the fundamentals of the Empire at school in Ceylon. Moreover the business I was handling at the bank established a direct connection for me between the country where I was living and the country of my birth. Having learned in my history lessons about the English East India Company and the Dutch East India Company (VOC), and seen concrete evidence of their deep influence around me while growing up in Ceylon, I was excited to be part of their world, however distantly in time. I was aware that both of these famous companies had once made economic and political history, and that in its heyday in the

*Headquarters of the Dutch East India Company in Bengal, c.1665.*

seventeenth-nineteenth centuries, the English East India Company—
generally known simply as *the* East India Company—was one of the
greatest companies the world had ever known.

\* \* \*

The key to understanding how European countries evolved organizations
like the East India Company, which was able to expand so dramatically
by making investments overseas using complex instruments of finance,
lies in the history of economics. Perhaps the most commonly used
definition of economics is still the one given by Lionel Robbins in 1932,
when he was a professor at the London School of Economics, in *An Essay
on the Nature and Significance of Economic Science*: "Economics is a
science which studies human behaviour as a relation between ends and
scarce means which have alternative uses." In other words, economists

recognize that there will always be too few resources to meet all the human demands upon those resources, and that both individuals and societies will choose to strike a balance between resources and demands in different ways that will vary at different periods in their history. For instance, capitalism and communism offer diametrically opposite, mutually exclusive solutions to the resource/demand problem. At the present moment throughout the world capitalism seems to have triumphed over most other solutions, including communism, by employing a prolific array of financial instruments. Without capitalism the paper world of finance as we know it would never have appeared.

*Babylonian silver loan contract tablet case made of fired clay, c.1820 BC.*

So in order to understand financial instruments, we need to trace the development of capitalism in the history of economics.

In the nineteenth century, and especially in the twentieth century, economists became a recognizable academic tribe, but one might say that economists have existed since ancient times, in the sense defined by Robbins, even if they did not call themselves economists. During the early period of Greek history, heroes, householders and landowners (with slaves) each took a different view of how best to employ resources. Merchants existed but were not much admired; it was considered inferior to obtain wealth by trade instead of by military exploits or agriculture.

*The cuneiform inscription records the loan of 9.33 grams of silver to Nabi-ilishu from the god Shamash and Sin-tajjar. The loan stipulates that the loan will be repaid at harvest time with interest.*

Opinions differed as to which of these two means to prosperity was the more fruitful—in contrast to Homer, Hesiod thought labour, honesty and peace would reap more benefits than heroism, deceit and war. Both poets, however, considered the ownership of land to be a vital contributor to material success.

Economics has always been closely connected with the political (and by extension the military) world. From about 594 BC, the Athenian statesman Solon introduced radical political changes, including debt cancellation and other reforms that stimulated trade and industry. He even divided the citizens of Athens into four classes based on their wealth, thus weakening the ruling aristocracy. The Athenian maritime trade expanded and goods like olive oil were exported in return for grain. This trend towards import-export continued into the Periclean Age (461–430 BC), as Roger Backhouse notes in *The Penguin History of Economics*: "trade flourished, and commercial agriculture and manufacturing developed, along with many of the activities now associated with a commercial society: banking, credit, money-changing, commodity speculation and monopoly trading." Hence the building of the Parthenon on the Athenian Acropolis in the Periclean period.

In the middle of the next century, Xenophon wrote a work that provides the origin of the word economics—*Oikonomikos*, a title which translates as 'Estate Management' or, more accurately, 'Household Management'. For Xenophon, wealth was the product of both efficient agricultural management and good political leadership. His ideas are still important because they emphasize a distinction between wealth arising from men working the land, which Xenophon regarded as a 'natural' activity, and wealth gained through trade and markets, which he regarded as peripheral. Xenophon's contemporary Plato agreed. "Though he saw a role for trade, the role for markets in his ideal state was very limited," writes Backhouse. "Consumer goods might be bought and sold, but property was to be allocated appropriately (on mathematical principles) between citizens. There would be no profits or payment of interest."

Plato's pupil Aristotle, though more concrete in his approach to economics than his idealist teacher, also distinguished between natural ways of obtaining money, such as agriculture, and unnatural ways, such as commerce and usury. Commerce was unacceptable to Aristotle because it offered apparently unlimited wealth.

Ancient Roman ideas on economics resembled those of ancient Greece in that war and conquest were regarded as acceptable means of acquiring wealth. Also, trade was considered to be tainted and unnatural as compared to landowning; financial gain needed to be converted into land in order to obtain political power in the Roman world. The Romans had great respect for property. This led them to develop a commercial legal system, and it is Roman jurisprudence that is the main Roman contribution to economic thought. It codified the idea of the corporation as an entity with an existence independent of its constituent members, for the first time. Roman commercial law covered contracts for trade, provided guarantees for property and facilitated the transfer of property—all within a framework of ideas relating to justice and morality. In fact, ancient classical ideas on economics were a powerful reason why economic debate would be inseparable from ethical issues until the seventeenth century.

The other major reason was religion, not surprisingly. However, the religious views of trade in the two monotheistic faiths, Christianity and Islam, differed substantively from those of ancient Greece and Rome.

The Old Testament distinguished between wealth pursued for its own sake, which was thought to encourage immoral practices, and wealth that materialized naturally from working hard and following God's commandments; and the New Testament and early Christianity took a similar view. St Augustine, writing in the fifth century after the sack of Rome, declared that wealth was a gift from God and that trade in itself was not bad; any possible sin would lie in the attitude of the trader, not in the act of trading. The Dominican friar St Thomas Aquinas, a major figure in scholastic economics in the thirteenth century, though much influenced by Aristotle, nevertheless argued that the acquisition of wealth through commerce could be moral if the wealth was used for charitable and just purposes. Moreover Aquinas allowed that justice did not require a seller, such as a grain merchant, to inform a potential buyer of all the circumstances relating to a sale, for instance the merchant's knowledge that another ship full of grain was about to arrive. "The just price was the price that was appropriate to the present, not the one that would prevail in the future," comments Backhouse. As for Islam, the Koran dictated that property and income should be taxed to support the poor. It also opposed the charging of interest on loans, which meant that Islamic finance would develop in a way different from the evolution of banking in the Christian West.

Ironically, the clash between Christianity and Islam in the Crusades was beneficial for European commerce; long-distance trade with the East expanded in the thirteenth century, led by Venice and other Italian financial and trading centres and facilitated by the political unity across Asia enforced by the Mongol Empire. But with the Muslim defeat of the Crusaders in the Holy Land near the end of the century and the revival of Moorish power in Spain, this commercial expansion ceased, long-distance trade lessened dramatically, and many of Europe's leading banking houses collapsed.

The fourteenth century was a generally turbulent time for Europeans. It witnessed a decline in the feudal order based on the high status of land given to courtiers in return for military service, and a rise in the status of the merchant class, which prompted the development of new forms of banking. In the middle of the century, in 1347–51, the Black Death killed a third of Europe's population, while in some areas as many as half of the inhabitants perished. Those peasants remaining were then in a strong position to demand wages for their labour, rather than serving their feudal lords in the old manner. Another economic fall-out of the Black Death was that rulers resorted to debasement of the currency by reducing the silver and gold content of coinage, in order to bolster their declining revenues.

During the next century and the one after, as the Italian Renaissance gathered pace, the most dramatic increases in European wealth came as a result of maritime exploration. New, ocean-based trading routes were established and the Spanish conquests in America resulted in vast amounts of silver and gold flooding into Europe. Mercantilism was born—the notion espoused by later economic writers that a nation's wealth, represented by its holdings of gold or bullion, depended upon its foreign trade, and that, for growth in wealth to occur, the balance of trade should favour exports over imports. Mercantilists believed in using the power of the state to intervene in order to maximize wealth. Mercantilism dominated European economic thought until the Enlightenment in the eighteenth century and went hand in hand with the birth of nation states. A typical mercantilist was Sir Thomas Smith, who in 1549 published *A Discourse of the Common Weal of This Realm of England*. This book broke with the ethical concerns of scholastic economics by accepting that men were motivated by self-interest to seek profits. Inflation, the sixteenth-century trend towards ever-rising prices—which was a new phenomenon in economic life—was, said Smith, only a problem for those on a fixed income, because both buyers and sellers gained from rising prices. A little before Smith, Niccolò Machiavelli had taken a similar view of human motives in politics in his famously cynical work on statecraft, *The Prince*, written in 1513, which argued that rulers were entitled to use cruelty and deception to strengthen the state. Thus, during the course of the sixteenth century, morality came to be increasingly divorced from politics and economics.

On 31 December 1600, in the City of London, the English East India Company was founded by a chartered company of merchants. Its formal name, until 1708, was the Governor and Company of Merchants of London Trading into the East Indies, and after this date the United Company of Merchants of England Trading to the East Indies, until it was finally wound up in 1873. Its foundation was quickly followed, in 1602, by its Dutch counterpart, the Vereenigde Nederlandsche

Geoctroyeerde Oostindische Compagnie (United Netherlands Chartered East India Company, or VOC), which survived until 1799. The importance of both companies lay "in the novel mechanism [they] offered for financing the exploration and commercial expansion of European business ventures around the globe," as William Goetzmann and Geert Rouwenhorst emphasize in *The Origins of Value*. Shareholders in these venture-capital companies took major risks with their money—with the prospect of commensurately massive profits if the trading voyages turned out successful. In the English East India Company, until 1612 each voyage was separately subscribed; thereafter temporary joint stocks were issued (four in all) until 1657, when a permanent joint stock was raised.

The original intention of the English East India Company had been to break the Dutch monopoly of the spice trade in the East Indies, in which the London merchants were unsuccessful. However, the English gained important trading posts in India, first in Surat in western India in 1608, then in Madras in 1639, then in Bombay (which was ceded to the company by the British Crown) in 1668, and finally in Calcutta in 1690. Although the English East India Company did not have a monopoly of Indian exports, by the early eighteenth century it had the largest share. The power of the Mughal Empire was now declining, threatening the trade and profits of Europeans and prompting the East India Company to become more involved in Indian politics. There was also rivalry between the English and the French East India companies, which eventually came to war in south India and ended with the British acquiring total control over India's international trade in the 1760s. A period of territorial expansion, intense exploitation and considerable corruption followed— the period of Robert Clive's military and political success in India—until the passing by the British government of the Regulating Act of 1773, which reformed the East India Company's practices and gained the government a share of the company's revenue. The appointment of a governor-general in Bengal marked the beginning of British official control of Indian affairs, which was increased by the India Act of 1784.

However, the company continued to control commercial activity in India, and it was not until 1833 that its monopoly was removed.

The success of the East India Company encouraged the English belief in mercantilism. In 1664, Thomas Mun's posthumously published *England's Treasure by Forraign Trade*, offered a theory of national growth centred on foreign trade, rather than indigenous productivity. "Mun's theory provided a justification for the East India Company, of which he was a director, being allowed to export bullion to India. This was necessary because the Company could not find suitable goods for export," notes Roger Backhouse. Despite increasing challenges from other economic ideas, economic thinking in this period remained dominated by concern for the balance of trade—the amount of revenue received from export once the cost of imports had been deducted.

The challenges arose from the more secular outlook of the late seventeenth century, the period of the founding of the Royal Society (in 1662) and the Bank of England (in 1694) and the start of the Scientific Revolution. In England, society was influenced by scientists like Sir Isaac Newton, who became Warden of the Mint in 1696, and the liberal political theorist John Locke, who also published on economics. Economic thought benefited from increased objectivity. In 1670, William Petty produced the first national accounts after detailed calculations based on reasonable assumptions about the population and resources. National income was defined by Petty as the total of the payments received from all sources of production: land, labour and capital. He also discussed the value of assets based on mathematical ratios between a range of factors, for example he took the ratio of rent to the value of land to be the same as the ratio of profits to the value of capital. By devising a workable economic model for the real world, Petty was able to suggest ways in which the nation could increase its wealth, such as the taxation of imports. His accounts were developed by Gregory King, who produced comparative accounts for England, France and Holland in 1688, at the time of the Dutch ruler William of Orange's accession to the English throne, and again in 1695, when England was at war with France. King calculated that the war would run out of funds in 1698 (peace was negotiated in 1697). However, it was not until the twentieth century that national accounts became reliable indicators of the value of a nation's wealth and assets.

Throughout history, as we have seen, economists have theorized about the idea of value, whether it be the value of commodities, of trade or of money. The purpose has always been to find the most effective means of increasing trade, profits and wealth by understanding their intricate inter-relationships and maintaining a correct balance between them. According to Locke's arguments in the late seventeenth century—published by him in 1668 when he was secretary to the Chancellor of the Exchequer in a pamphlet titled *Some Consequences That are Like to Follow upon Lessening of Interest to 4 per cent*—money's value depended on the quantity of money in relation to trade. Too much money in circulation would reduce its value and raise the price of commodities, which would reduce trade. In an isolated economy, if the money supply were reduced, prices would fall and trade would be stimulated. But if his theory was to work in a world of international trade, Locke thought that each country would need to have a similar ratio of money to trade—if one country's home prices were less than another's, the first country would lose out by paying more for its imports than its income from its exports. The interest rates for lending and borrowing money therefore interested Locke very much, as a mechanism for controlling money and trade. He thought interest rates were dependent on the amount of money a nation had available for trade. His firm view was that low interest rates were a product of wealth rather than a generator of wealth; they reduced the quantity of money available for lending.

In 1695, during the recoinage crisis of that decade, Locke had a chance

*John Locke's economic arguments, published in 1668, stated that money's value depended on the quantity of money in relation to trade.*

to test part of his theories in the real economy. English silver coins had become seriously debased in size through the illegal practice of clipping (milled edges around coins were invented at this time to prevent this); since the Restoration of Charles II in 1660, silver coins had contained progressively less silver. Locke advocated—and the government adopted—a scheme, (which would be fanatically supervised by Newton at the Mint), whereby the government would recoin silver shillings with their full complement of silver, while agreeing to exchange old shillings for new ones over a period of six months. The immediate result was that people grabbed large numbers of the more valuable new shillings, melted them down and exported the silver, causing the value of silver shillings in circulation to drop from an estimated £12 million in December 1695 to a mere £4.2 million in June 1696. The money supply was thus severely reduced, and prices fell, as Locke had predicted. A more significant effect of the overvaluation of silver coins, though, was that they continued to be scarcer than before the recoinage, and eventually England moved away from silver and on to a gold standard for its paper currency.

Behind the government's scheme, and Locke's ideas, lay the very important assumption that the (face) value of money should be determined by the (commodity) value of its metal. For mercantilist thought insisted that the amount of bullion held by a country represented its wealth. As Backhouse clearly explains, "it was gold and silver that were the instruments of commerce. They had an intrinsic value determined by common consent. The only thing that was different about money was that it contained a stamp containing its weight and fineness." But some other economists of the time, such as Nicholas Barbon, opposed this assumption, and argued that money had a value independent of its metal content, backed by people's faith in the government that issued the money. In other words, Barbon espoused the same view that had prevailed in the China of the Song dynasty, with its iron and paper currency. Today, of course, this latter view rules the economic roost, and is the reason why banknotes and other more sophisticated instruments of finance exercise their extraordinary power.

Although the Bank of England and its banknotes were still in their infancy, John Law's *Money and Trade Considered: A Proposal for Supplying the Nation with Money*, published in Edinburgh in 1705, argued that paper currency should be expanded. The use of paper would make the control of the money supply both easier and cheaper than the use of metal—which would stabilize the currency. Law proposed that paper money be valued against land rather than silver, which he claimed had the more stable value. But Law, who is a key figure in the history of economics, did not get to see his proposals adopted in his native Scotland, for he was forced into exile in 1706 in order to avoid being arrested for murder. (He had killed a man in a duel in England in 1694, fled to the Continent, and then returned to Scotland, but the prospective union of England and Scotland in 1707 rendered him liable to prosecution at home.) However Law achieved a position of influence in France, his country of exile, after the death of the financially ruinous Louis XIV in 1715. He established a bank with paper currency, which became the Royal Bank of France, and a trading company, and was made Controller-General of Finances in 1720. His idea was that the banknotes would be accepted as payment of taxes, but the scheme ran aground in financial crises and was finally scuppered by a plague outbreak in which people lost faith in paper and demanded coinage. Paper money was still viewed with suspicion, both by the populace and by most economists. Thus, David Hume, the philosopher and historian, writing on economics in 1752, opposed paper money because he thought it would tend to increase the amount of money in circulation, thereby raising prices and driving manufacturing abroad where it was cheaper, without having the offsetting benefit of raising the state's store of gold and silver, a precious reserve for use in times of war. It would take until the second half of the nineteenth century before paper money would dominate the finances of any country.

With the gradual waning in the eighteenth century of religious explanations of phenomena, the human motivations behind economic activity were increasingly the subject of investigation. Ideas on the subject varied widely—just as the ideas of today's economists do! For example, in 1714, in his notoriously amoral *The Fable of the Bees: or Private Vices turned Public Benefits*, Bernard Mandeville argued that while producers and consumers (the individual bees in the hive) were naturally selfish, their lust for luxury voluntarily created prosperity for the whole of society (the hive itself)—even burglars provided employment for locksmiths. Hence, private vices produced public benefits. In contrast, Francis Hutcheson, generally regarded as the founder of the Scottish Enlightenment, attributed a mixture of motives to people, including altruism, as well as undoubted self-interest. Hutcheson argued that spending on luxury goods was not the engine of prosperity, since people were inclined to ensure that their fellows had necessary goods before seeking their own luxuries. Hume, by contrast, favoured the importance of luxury spending, but not for the same reasons as Mandeville. Hume's stance was that wealth was based on labour, and labour would only be undertaken when there was an incentive to do so. Luxury spending was a vital incentive to make people work and lift them out of a subsistence economy.

But what was the proper role of the state in creating this incentive? A group of eighteenth-century French economists came up with a key idea. Led by the physician of Louis XV, François Quesnay, they became known as physiocrats. Like physicians, physiocrats believed that the economic pathologies of society must be cured by working with nature not against it. They therefore extolled agriculture over commerce, against the ideas of the mercantilists. Agriculture was virtuous and natural, physiocrats argued, because agriculture, unlike manufacturing and trade, on top of a financial surplus also produced a surplus of goods. The way to encourage agriculture was, generally speaking, to leave it alone, with little government intervention. "Taxation, interference with agriculture, artificial stimulation of manufacturing, keeping food prices low—all policies pursued by the governments of Louis XIV and Louis XV—were all harmful and should be abandoned," writes Backhouse of the physiocratic political agenda. Physiocrats stressed the necessity of free trade, and became associated with the influential concept of laissez-faire economics. (However, the phrase *laissez faire, laissez passer* was actually made popular not by a physiocrat but by a businessman then in government, Vincent de Gournay, sympathetic to the physiocrats though not entirely in agreement with their political agenda.)

Two more phrases important in today's economics—'political economy' and 'supply and demand'—appeared in a book published in 1767 by Sir James Steuart. Its title and subtitle, exhaustive in the manner of the day, were as follows: *An Inquiry into the Principles of Political Oeconomy: Being an Essay on the Science of Domestic Policy in Free Nations, in which are Particularly Considered Population, Agriculture, Trade, Industry, Money, Coin, Interest, Circulation, Banks, Exchange, Public Credit and Taxes*. Steuart's book may be said to be the first systematic study of economics written in English. However it was soon eclipsed by Adam Smith's seminal *An Inquiry into the Nature and Causes of the Wealth of Nations*, published in 1776.

Smith, a student of Hutcheson, had followed his old teacher by becoming professor of moral philosophy at Glasgow University in 1752, where he published his much reprinted book, *The Theory of Moral Sentiments*. After this, in 1764–66, he travelled in France as a tutor to a Scottish duke, where he was introduced to Quesnay and other physiocrats. His economic writings developed the physiocratic idea of laissez-faire, and laid the foundations for the entire subsequent school of English classical economics.

Smith thought that wealth could be increased by the division of labour: instead of a man working to make a product on his own, he could specialize in doing one part of the job of production as a member of a team, improving efficiency and output, as in a modern factory. Smith's ideas took account of manufacturing as well as agriculture, reflecting the growing industrialization of British society during the century. The value of goods was related to their labour input; the price of goods was dependent on supply and demand. Although Smith considered individuals to be selfish and idle by nature, he knew they were motivated to create their own wealth. In Smith's view, the pursuit of wealth, though motivated by selfish aims, would cause individuals to be led as if by an 'invisible hand' to benefit society as a whole. In his own words, in *The Theory of Moral Sentiments*: "Society may subsist among different men, as among different merchants, from a sense of its utility, without any mutual love or affection; and though no man in it should owe any obligation, or be bound in gratitude to any other, it may still be upheld by a mercenary exchange of good offices according to an agreed valuation." But for this process to operate, Smith stressed that free-market competition between individuals was necessary—a minimum of government intervention, as in the laissez-faire policy of the physiocrats. A commercial society would flourish with government laissez-faire, Smith asserted, however he did recognize that this would require at least some constraints on human ruthlessness, chiefly a legal framework for dispensing justice. He commented: "Society may subsist, though not in the most comfortable state, without beneficence; but the prevalence of injustice must utterly destroy it."

Smith's primary concern in *The Wealth of Nations* was economic growth. He saw growth as the expansion of markets: the larger a market was, the greater the scope for division of labour and specialist production. But the labour had to be of the right kind, that is 'productive labour'—labour that added value to something, such as farm labour, and hence accumulated capital—in contrast to 'unproductive labour', such as that of a menial servant (or indeed a judge or an economist). In a competitive society, individuals were at liberty to move their capital and labour from one activity to another so as to produce whatever was in demand. It was for this reason that Smith opposed the mercantilist

*Adam Smith's seminal book* An Inquiry into the Nature and Causes of the Wealth of Nations *was published in 1776.*

restrictions on trade, notably the East India Company's trade monopoly controlled and taxed by the government—they hindered free trade with tariffs and trade wars. If individuals and companies could compete freely, they would find a natural demand for their services.

The French Revolution, which began the year before Smith's death in 1790, moved economics away from moral philosophy and entangled it inextricably with politics. Britain's war with France, which broke out in 1793, caused acute economic difficulties in Britain. There was a financial crisis in 1797, which was what forced the Bank of England to suspend the convertibility of sterling into gold and Britain to remain on a paper currency until 1819, as mentioned in chapter one. During that period, the number of banknotes issued by the Bank of England increased and prices rose. The bank's directors defended their policy by saying that the value of banknotes in circulation was unrelated to the price of bullion

According to their so-called 'real-bills doctrine', so long as a bank lent money against 'real bills'—in other words bills for financing genuine commercial transactions rather than speculation—the bills would simply be repaid on completion of the transaction. The assumption was that people would only borrow money and pay interest on it if their transactions were necessary and genuine. But as Henry Thornton pointed out in 1802, in *An Inquiry into the Nature and Effects of the Paper Credit*, the assumption was flawed: speculators might well choose to borrow if the interest rate on a loan were less than the rate of profit obtainable on a speculation—thereby inflating the number of banknotes in circulation and pushing up prices.

Events in France and harsh economic times at home undoubtedly influenced the theories of Thomas Malthus, a clergyman economist opposed to the forcible redistribution of property and resources advocated by radicals on both sides of the English Channel in order to give everyone decent living conditions. Malthus's small tract, *Essay on the Principle of Population*, published anonymously in 1798, argued that England's rising population would always outstrip food supplies, and so improved living standards for all were an impossibility. Since resources were finite, and the population was increasing, the poor must be left to fend for themselves, while being encouraged not to breed by birth control measures. Giving state money to them (under the Poor Laws) only increased their dependence on others, rather than developing their survival skills. Malthus was influential in nineteenth-century politics (and remains so in our current fears about over-population), but his views provoked massive opposition—not only from humanitarians but also from a utilitarian philosopher like Jeremy Bentham, who countered Malthus with the idea that an action was morally correct if it produced the "greatest happiness of the greatest number".

In the generation after Smith, David Ricardo was the most prominent economist. He had little formal education but was the son of Jewish parents connected with the money market, in which he too worked from the age of 14. Ricardo made a fortune, and this enabled him to retire at the age of 42 in 1814. Soon after this, in 1817, he published his most significant work, *The Principles of Political Economy and Taxation*. It attempted to analyze how wealth was distributed.

Ricardo considered the value of a commodity to be dependent on the amount of labour required to produce it, and went on to examine three factors in production: wages, profit and rent. As a theoretical model he used corn (wheat) production, and assumed that the population and customary subsistence level of labourers would rise, producing a rising level of demand. He allowed more and more land to be cultivated until eventually unsuitable land had to be used, leading to a fall in profits, expressed by the law of diminishing returns. Like many economic models, its realism was limited by its theoretical basis. Had real labourers agreed to eat only corn, as the theory assumed, the model might have been workable, but human behaviour cannot be prescribed so closely.

Nevertheless, Ricardo's use of a theoretical model set a trend for economists wishing to introduce rigour, including mathematics, into their analyses. Among those owing a real debt to him was Karl Marx, who used Ricardo's theories in his major work of 1867, *Das Kapital*, in order to analyze capitalism critically. (It is an irony, given Marx's famous preoccupation with the capitalist exploitation of workers, that his analysis of the business cycle, the periodic booms and busts, in terms of fixed-capital accumulation, turned out to be useful to twentieth-century economists examining business-cycle theory in terms of the relations between saving and investment.) Furthermore, Ricardo's work on international trade survives even today in his theory or law of comparative advantage. This states that it may still be profitable for a country to make a product (e.g. wine) even though that product can be made more cheaply in another country, provided that there is a second product (e.g. cloth) for which the reverse is true. The two countries can then exchange the two products, wine and cloth, profitably within a certain range of prices, since each country has a comparative advantage over the other, depending on the product. Ricardo's comparative advantage theory underpinned the case for free trade, in line with Adam Smith's thinking.

*The Principles of Political Economy and Taxation* dominated English classical economics for half a century. By the time its influence began to wane, in the last decades of the nineteenth century, economics had become professionalized; it was now an academic discipline, debating issues of supply and demand, production and value, while developing theoretical models. Central to economic discussion in this period was the idea of utility—the pleasure or satisfaction an individual derives from being part of a particular situation or from consuming goods or services—and the question of whether utility could be measured. How did utility relate to value? Ricardo had argued that although an item must have a utility to have a value, its value could be measured simply by its production cost without reference to its utility. Léon Walras, a former mining engineer appointed as the first professor of economics at Lausanne University in 1870, thought value depended on scarcity. By contrast, William Jevons, a former assayer at the Australian Mint appointed professor of political economy at University College, London in 1876, thought value was entirely dependent on utility. While Ricardo's clear-cut definition of value was plainly inadequate, neither of the other two definitions was fully satisfactory or easily measurable. Although Walras and Jevons were knowledgeable mathematicians, they had the good sense to appreciate the limitations of mathematics when applied to many economic concepts.

Alfred Marshall, who was professor of political economy at Cambridge University from 1885–1908, became the leading figure in British economics from the 1880s, after the publication of his book *The Economics of Industry*, until around 1930; his 1890 textbook, *Principles of Economics*, went through multiple editions and was still used as late as the 1950s. Marshall employed utility theory to explain supply and demand. Instead of studying overarching issues such as growth, inflation and unemployment (known as macro-economics), Marshall focused on individual markets (micro-economics). He invented mathematical supply and demand curves and applied them to different kinds of product— say, perishable and storeable goods. He drew a distinction between the amount of money consumers were prepared to pay for a particular quantity of a product and the amount they had to pay in reality, as dictated by the market price. He also took the effect of time into account by considering supply and demand over four periods: the market period (during which no more product could be produced), the short run (over which production and employment levels could be changed, but not skilled labour or machinery), the long run (over which firms had the time to reorganize, retrain and retool to meet new demands), and finally the very long run (in which there were secular movements in price, caused by long-term developments in, for instance, population, education, technological knowledge and capital). Although Marshall had trained as a mathematician, he was healthily sceptical about mathematics in economics. "He wanted economics to be realistic," writes Roger Backhouse, "but the use of mathematics made it very easy to derive results that had no foundation in reality. If mathematical results could not be translated into English, he was suspicious of them." Nevertheless, since Marshall's time, economics has become increasingly mathematical, and many of its theories incredibly complex.

The most accessible and significant economist of the twentieth century, widely credited as the founder of macro-economics, was John Maynard Keynes. He captured attention in Britain after the First World War when he resigned from the Treasury team at the 1919 Versailles peace conference to write *The Economic Consequences of the Peace*, and described the reparations being pursued by the victorious Allies against the defeated Germany as damaging to the international economy. But his major work, *The General Theory of Employment, Interest and Money*, was published in 1936. Like most economic theory it was influenced by the prevailing climate, which was then one of economic depression and

*The most accessible and significant economist of the twentieth century, widely credited as the founder of macro-economics, was John Maynard Keynes.*

unemployment. Keynes argued that full employment was not necessary for a stable economy; however, unemployment could be reduced if governments chose to increase public spending and reduce taxation. These measures would create demand in the economy, and therefore jobs. Keynes's theories were remarkably popular, guiding the post-war welfare state in Britain and influencing Western political economic thought for a generation after his death in 1946. Only in the 1970s, with rising inflation, did Keynesian policies fall out of favour, and a new economic theory—monetarism—gradually take their place.

Economists came to exert tangible influence on national economies at this time, partly as a result of their role in military strategy and tactics during the Second World War. In 1940, Keynes even wrote a book entitled *How to Pay for the War*. Their thinking and their mathematical techniques were of real value in choosing alternative ways to allocate scarce wartime resources. Would more resources be saved by increasing production of a particular weapon and using it against the enemy than were used up in making the weapon? Such thinking could be redeployed after the war into solving peacetime economic issues, such as how to promote economic reconstruction and growth.

Between the two world wars, the League of Nations employed economists who contributed to economic reconstruction after 1918; from 1944 onwards, such economists worked for the International Monetary Fund (IMF) and the World Bank. The IMF's aims were to encourage international monetary cooperation, stabilize exchange rates, expand world trade and get rid of foreign-exchange restrictions. In the 1970s and after, it gave financial help to countries in trouble, including Britain, conditional on a country's agreeing to adopt specified reforms of its economy. The World Bank served a similar purpose, advising and lending money to developing countries. Both organizations have been criticized for giving inappropriate advice and exacerbating national problems. The World Trade Organisation (WTO), another powerful international economic body, was set up in Geneva in 1995 following the Uruguay round of trade negotiations to replace the 1948 General Agreement on Tariffs and Trade. It, too, has been attacked, this time for establishing rules for world trade beneficial to rich countries at the expense of poorer ones. As a result, in all three of these powerful organizations—the IMF, the World Bank and the WTO—there is now a greater recognition than there was in the post-war decades, that lending and trade must take real account of how to increase the welfare of nations, not just the bank balances of the well off (and the corrupt). To measure the welfare of a community, economists are increasingly compelled to go beyond such measures as per capita national income or gross national product and focus on how goods are distributed within a society. A key question has become, not only how to maximize growth, but also how to allocate resources efficiently.

Regardless of the rights and wrongs of these three organizations' economic policies, what is indisputable is that their very existence demonstrates the consolidation of world capitalism. International trade and economic thought have come a long way over the past four centuries since the foundation of the East India Company and have culminated in a global financial system driven by the supporters of free trade and capitalism. As a result, the world of economics and the world of finance—with its paper financial instruments—are totally interdependent.

Looked at from the financial point of view, the most remarkable thing about the East India Company was that it was not a limited-liability company. As a joint-stock company, it had transferable shares, but each of its shareholders—who admittedly were very wealthy men—would be liable for the entire losses of the company, were one of its ships to be impounded by the Dutch, or be robbed of its cargo by pirates en route from the East to London, or suffer shipwreck and fail to return altogether. Not until as late as 1855, less than 20 years before the East India Company was wound up, was limited liability legislated for in Britain to protect shareholders against potentially ruinous losses, should their company become insolvent. In a limited-liability company, the maximum sum ordinary shareholders can forfeit as result of insolvency is the original capital they invested in the company. This new assurance of reduced risk changed the thinking of investors and indeed the psychology behind corporate finance. Limited liability, notes the author of a recent *Financial Times Guide to Investing*, was "one of the most important breakthroughs in the development of UK capitalism and economic progress". As the *Economist* magazine commented in 1999 in its millennial issue, "The modern world is built on two centuries of industrialization. Most of that was built by equity finance. Which is built on limited liability."

The concept of the corporation—with partners and a permanent existence independent of the identity of the partners—can be traced back to the Romans, as mentioned before; its Latin name was a *societas publicanorum* ('society of publicans'). But there is no evidence, at least in the time of the Roman Republic, that the Roman law governing the *societas* included limited liability. In modern times, limited liability first appeared in Continental Europe and in the United States in the eighteenth century in the form of limited partnerships, where at least one partner was totally liable but the other partners were liable only for the capital they had invested in the business. There were also successful limited-liability banks in Scotland. But it was in the United States that the full-fledged concept took off. In 1811, the state of New York was the first US state to introduce a general limited-liability law for manufacturing companies. It was popular; other states followed; and there was a flight of capital to states with limited liability from states without it, which prompted most American states to introduce a similar law by 1830.

It seems surprising, given the Industrial Revolution in Britain and the growth of manufacturing companies in this period, that Britain did not lead the way with limited liability. But strong voices had been raised against it, including those of Adam Smith and John Stuart Mill, voices who claimed that limiting liability would "create excessive speculation, create difficulties in securing credit, and promote fraudulent investment schemes"—as noted by William Carney in a detailed discussion of the history of limited liability. Supporters of limited liability, who included Victorian philanthropists seeking to invest the savings of working people safely—argued that its introduction would encourage the expansion of major businesses, notably the construction of railways, housing and factories, which would ultimately prove beneficial to society as a whole. In the end, the government's need to encourage cautious wealthy investors, combined with Victorian confidence in free enterprise, carried the day. Even so, the implementation of limited liability in Britain was slow compared with the United States. Thirty years after its introduction in Britain in 1855, only ten per cent of the English firms generally regarded as important were incorporated as limited-liability companies.

Although the Roman *societas* may have been the first ever business to use transferable shares, the Roman system had no lasting influence on commerce and finance. The first instance of shares and share dividend payments enjoying wide use is generally attributed to the various East India companies founded in the seventeenth century, which certainly left a lasting legacy in the paper world. The initial share capital of the Dutch East India Company, the VOC, was ten times that of the English East India Company, so inevitably it had the greater effect of the two companies on the history of shareholding.

To begin with, from 1602, VOC shareholders who felt disappointed by their dividends were entitled to withdraw from the enterprise and be repaid their share capital intact. In 1609, however, the directors of the VOC, who were the chief shareholders, changed this policy and "declared the capital to be non-refundable," writes Larry Neal in his

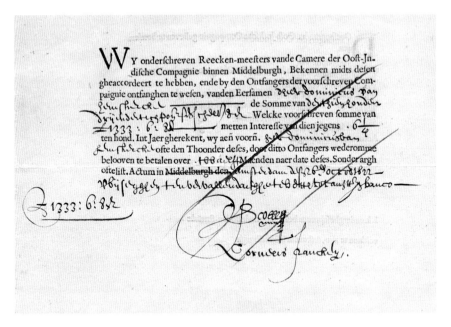

*Bond of the Dutch East India Company founded in 1602. The line through the text indicates that the debt was repaid.*

study of the Dutch company in *The Origins of Value*, "so disappointed shareholders from then on had no recourse but to sell their shares to someone else," if they wanted to get their hands on cash. "Liquidity, in turn, depended on the size and diversity of the customer base for the asset and the quantity of shares available for transfer."

It is not hard to see how this situation would lead to the development of stock exchanges for buying and selling shares—at first in Europe, later in America, then around the world. In the early seventeenth century, there was a thriving trade in VOC shares on the Amsterdam Exchange, and they were the dominant trade by the end of the century. The Dutch influence on British trading in shares of all kinds was strengthened when Prince William of Orange became King William III of England in 1689; many Dutch financial practices were later adopted in Britain.

In London, shares were initially traded informally in the flourishing coffee houses of the City, such as New Jonathan's. Then in 1773 (the year that the government first regulated the English East India Company), a group of brokers got together and purchased a building in Threadneedle Street near the Bank of England, which they opened as a stock exchange with membership by subscription and rules for trading. In 1801, 500 traders broke away from this exchange after a dispute over the rules and opened their own exchange close by at Capel Court, which was formally constituted in 1802. By the 1840s, hundreds of different company shares were listed on the exchange. Two markets in due course developed in the London Stock Exchange: the primary market, where companies sell newly issued shares to investors, and the secondary market, where existing shares are traded. The two are interdependent, in that the secondary market clearly depends on the success of the primary market, while a reliable and liquid secondary market—one that has sufficient buyers and sellers to function effectively—is needed to encourage investment in the primary market.

With the huge growth in trading, other institutions mushroomed alongside stock exchanges. Today, investment or merchant banks make many millions from managing share portfolios for investors, as well as from handling company mergers and share issues. With share issues, these banks conduct the preparatory work on behalf of the company issuing the new shares, and promote the issue by backing it with their reputation. They research other relevant and competitor companies, by investigating the exact nature of their businesses, their relationship with their suppliers, the track record of their directors, their published accounts, their history and past performance, their plans and their prospects; and they coordinate with the brokers, underwriters, accountants and solicitors who will actually sell the new shares. Finally, they produce a detailed printed prospectus attractive to investors inviting them to put capital into the company by buying the new shares. In the stock market, each investment requires its own particular research. In general, it is research that makes the difference between an investment decision taken with a reasonable amount of risk, and pure speculation.

Company annual reports contain balance sheets summarizing total assets, liabilities and net assets, cash flow statements, directors' reports and a chairman's statement on recent and future performance. A potential investor should be able to look at the report and accounts, easily compare turnover from one year with turnover from another, and determine how any increase was achieved and where the operating profit came from. The accounts should not be difficult to understand. If they are, the company may well be untrustworthy and should be avoided, in the view of Warren Buffett, one of the world's super-successful investors. Another highly successful investor, Peter Lynch, advises: "Go for a business that any idiot can run—because sooner or later, any idiot probably is going to run it."

The capital structure of a company is also vitally important, that is, its proportion of debt to equity. This figure indicates whether the company is doing well enough to consider financial leverage (gearing), in other words whether it has the power to borrow more money for further investment. Borrowing can take various forms, such as bank loans, share issues and bond issues, but in every case the company will need to persuade its lenders and shareholders as well as other investors that the proposed expansion offers a worthwhile risk. If the company already has substantial debts, which must be serviced regardless of its performance, outsiders may decide that further borrowing would not be prudent. Here a successful investor, besides knowledge of the company, needs a certain amount of vision to imagine how its future could unfold.

A share certificate is nothing but a piece of paper, yet the market places a value on it. In many ways, shares (also known as equities, or stocks in the United States) might seem to be an offputting form of investment. Obviously, no investor can guarantee the future success of a company, so share-owning always carries a certain amount of risk, and the risk is sometimes unquantifiable. Furthermore, if profits are made, the company is under no legal obligation to pay the shareholders a proportion of the profits as a dividend, unlike its legal obligation to pay contractually agreed interest on its debt to a bank or other lender. If the company is liquidated, shareholders are the last in a long list of creditors to be paid, well behind banks and bondholders, in fact as a rule shareholders do not get reimbursed by insolvent companies—unless they own so-called preference shares (known as preferred stock in the US), rather than the more usual ordinary shares. However, shareholders do have some valuable rights. They jointly own all the value a company creates once it has paid what it owes, and as its owners, shareholders can vote on how the company is being, or should be, managed. The more shares they own, the more votes they have. Thus shareholders can influence company mergers and the appointment of company directors. In Britain, they are also offered a proportion of any new shares issued, based on the percentage of the shares they already own.

My personal choice of shares was for preference shares, as we shall see later. This was partly because they are more secure in the event of insolvency, but also because preference shares pay fixed dividends quarterly, ahead of the dividends paid to ordinary shareholders. The disadvantage of preference shares over ordinary shares is that they do not usually have voting rights, and do not participate in ordinary share growth. (However, 'convertible' preference shares that can be converted into ordinary shares obviate that disadvantage.)

Share prices are set in the same way as other goods in the market place: by supply and demand. If there is news—or merely a rumour—of a company's poor performance in any respect, demand for the company's shares falls and its share price drops accordingly. Although the number of shares issued by a company is determined by its net assets, the true value of the share depends not only on the company's net assets but also on the company's future growth or contraction. This, needless to say, cannot be predicted with certainty. So the true value of a share may differ substantially from its market price. I have made a considerable amount of money from careful research into companies with shares having a low price-to-earnings ratio, that I judged to be seriously undervalued.

Apart from shares, bonds are the other extremely widespread form of paper investment. In 2002, 73 per cent of the British government's debt comprised bonds—known as gilts—totalling £273 billion. *The Financial Times Guide to Investing* claims that bonds are "the most significant financial instruments in the world today, with over $37 trillion in issue". Bonds are much less risky than shares. A bondholder's money is lent either to a company (corporate bonds) or to a government (government bonds or gilts). In exchange, bondholders receive IOU coupons that remain in force until the date of maturity. Unlike shares, a bondholder's capital is therefore usually secure and he is guaranteed a return on his capital, but the return is lower than for shares, as is usual in the world of investment—the higher the risk, the greater the potential return. But, just as with shares, there is a thriving secondary market in bonds, mainly in gilts rather than corporate bonds. There are many other types of bonds too: junk bonds (corporate bonds of low-quality security backing), which carry a high risk and are volatile, and therefore offer a higher return than government bonds; foreign bonds, for lending money to companies and governments in countries different from the bondholder's place of residence; and Eurobonds, which have nothing to do with the euro currency but are bonds issued in one country in the currency of another country. The attraction of Eurobonds is that they avoid taxes as well as the rules and regulations laid down by the London Stock Exchange.

There are countless other types of financial securities—a term which covers any medium of investment in the money or capital markets. For example, unit trusts function in a similar manner to shares, except that they are 'open-ended', meaning that the size of the fund and therefore the number of units available for purchase can be increased—hence the number of units can change daily, unlike with shares. Since the 1980s, one of the most important financial instruments has been the derivative, such as the option and the future. Derivatives function in two basic ways: either so as to reduce risk, or to act as a potentially high-return investment. Essentially derivatives are assets of which the performance is based on other underlying assets. There is nothing new about them in principle; they have been around since classical times. In ancient Greece, olive growers entered into forward agreements with buyers to fix the price of a forthcoming crop and its delivery date. This reduced the risk for both parties by removing uncertainty caused by price fluctuations and uncertainty about delivery and availability. Like many other financial instruments, derivatives are contracts giving the purchaser the right to buy or sell an underlying asset or to benefit from any rise or fall in its value. A derivative therefore acquires its own value and becomes an asset which can be traded. As early as the Middle Ages, there was a secondary market in forward contracts for wheat.

Options have existed for many years too; tulip options were traded in seventeenth-century Amsterdam. Option contracts give one party a right to buy or sell an underlying asset at a given price on or before a certain date, without obliging the party to take up the option. This encourages business by giving companies the right to expand in particular directions if on the specified future date they decide it is still beneficial for them to

*Tulipmania: a "chariot of fools" heads for the sea and almost certain disaster.*

do so. For example, by taking options on several pieces of land, one can later exercise an option to buy the most profitable one. Because the value of the underlying assets changes, options themselves become traded assets. Futures resemble options in that two parties agree to proceed with a transaction at a particular price on a particular date, but unlike with options, both the parties to a futures deal are fully committed to buy and sell. Futures have existed since the seventeenth century when they were used in Japan's rice market in Osaka.

Many other investment opportunities work by pooling the funds of multiple investors and putting the funds into shares, corporate bonds, gilts or property. Multiple permutations exist: an investor can manage his own funds or have a fully managed portfolio; investments can be fixed or flexible, regulated or unregulated; there can be a high or a low level of risk. Pooled funds include exchange-traded funds, with-profits policies, stock market-linked bonds, hedge funds and open-ended investment companies. Many investment vehicles also offer the opportunity for compounding, in other words generating interest on interest. Some of these vehicles are incredibly powerful. With hedge funds a small number of wealthy individuals each pool a large sum in a fund that bets on the movement of currencies, interest rates and other key financial indicators. Hedge funds are often located offshore, so as to be free from regulation, and they are frequently blamed for destabilizing markets by instantaneously moving billions from one part of the world to another— as the financier George Soros did when he bet against sterling in 1992 and made a billion dollars.

But while the choice of financial instruments seems endless and growing, it remains true that without the stock markets they would be useless. Over 100 countries now have stock markets, including Russia and China. These markets are in competition with one another, particularly those in New York and London. In 1986, the London Stock Exchange (LSE) was forced to introduce a number of startling reforms to bring it in line with the exchanges in New York, Tokyo and Frankfurt— so radical, in fact, that the change became known as  Big Bang. Until then, the LSE had functioned more like a club than a business, with the members protecting their own interests more than those of investors. Fraud might have been uncommon, but insider dealing, in which a handful of investors with private knowledge of a company's business plans use this privileged information to buy and sell shares ahead of the company's public announcement, was well known, though illegal. The 1986 reforms removed fixed broker commissions, opened up the ownership of the market makers (the organizations that trade in shares), made the LSE a public limited company and, most dramatically, removed the trading floor and replaced it with a computer system. Large financial conglomerates took over the market makers, the LSE's traditionally high interest rates dropped, shares were traded on the secondary market, and the LSE thrived. There is still some insider dealing, though, as the Financial Services Authority, the government's official regulator, was obliged to admit in a report published in 2006.

The LSE publishes the daily FTSE (Financial Times and Stock Exchange) 100 share index, representing Britain's 100 largest listed shares. *The Financial Times Guide to Investing* gives an indication of the level of finance involved in these companies in the primary market: "In 2002 alone UK-listed firms on the LSE raised new capital amounting to £103.4 billion by selling equity and fixed interest securities." In the secondary market, "On a typical day over 100,000 bargains (trades between buyers and sellers) are struck between investors in UK shares, worth over £7 billion." In addition, the AIM (Alternative Investment Market) lists 700 smaller and younger companies' share prices.

The LSE is now the largest stock exchange in the world for trading in overseas companies, but the New York Stock Exchange (NYSE) is the world's largest stock exchange. At the end of 2002, the market value of US domestic stocks listed there was $9,040 billion—a lot more than in Tokyo, the second largest stock exchange, with a market value of $2,076 billion. Unlike the LSE, which is a public limited company, the NYSE was a non-profit corporation controlled by its members and board of directors right up to 8 March 2006 when it became a publicly traded entity merging with the Archipelago Exchange. Trading works through a system of specialists and brokers, some of whom have become legendary figures. Among the most famous NYSE brokers was Jesse Livermore, who ran away from home in 1891, aged fourteen, with only five dollars, and went on to make, and lose, four fortunes on the New York stock market. A fanatically secretive trader working out of a highly secure Manhattan apartment, Livermore's technique involved short selling the market—speculating on borrowed shares, the price of which he expected to fall. In 1907, he made three million dollars in one day during a stock-market crash and J. P. Morgan personally begged him to stop. Livermore managed to survive the Wall Street crash of 1929 and entered the

*John Pierpont Morgan Jr., an enormous influence on Wall Street from the 1880s until his death in 1913.*

depression of the 1930s with over $100 million, but in 1940 he shot himself in a New York hotel. His book, *How to Trade in Stocks*, is considered a classic of finance, still relevant today.

Keynes referred to the fortunes gained and lost in the financial markets as "casino capitalism". He also came up with "animal spirits" as a phrase to describe the confidence of entrepreneurs necessary for economic prosperity—a kind of naïve, and sometimes predatory, optimism that leads them to succeed. Keynes wrote memorably that, "the thought of ultimate loss which often overtakes pioneers, as experience undoubtedly tells us and them, is put aside as a healthy man puts aside the expectation of death." In the financial world, the pioneers are the venture capitalists who back entrepreneurs. Venture capitalists may receive returns of between five and ten times their initial equity investment in as little as five years, or they may face financial disaster. Out of ten venture-capital investments, it is thought that two will be exceptional, two will fail completely and the other six will range from poor to good. There is no past performance to guide the investment decision—but as Warren Buffett says, "If past history was all there was to the game, the richest people would be librarians."

Buffett's wealth is now valued at $44 billion, second only to Microsoft's Bill Gates, who has joined the board of Buffett's investment company Berkshire Hathaway. It is estimated that one thousand dollars invested in Berkshire Hathaway in 1965 would be worth nearly three million today. However, Buffett is not infallible; he recently made financial news by losing $310 million betting against the US dollar. At his company's annual meeting in 2005, Buffett expressed concern over US trade and budget deficits. He also pointed to a global lack of enthusiasm for the US dollar which he thought might be due to many countries being flooded with dollars, and commented that it was hard to envisage a future with an appreciating US dollar. He also revealed that he was

*One thousand dollars invested in Warren Buffet's Berkshire Hathaway Inc. in 1965 would be worth nearly three million today.*

holding far more cash than in previous years as he struggled to identify good investments at a fair price.

What is the difference between risky investment like Buffett's and the mere speculation of a Livermore? *The Penguin Dictionary of Economics* defines risk as: "A state in which the number of possible future events exceeds the number of events that will actually occur, and some measure of probability can be attached to them." In this sense financial investing is somewhat like gambling where the odds are known, probabilities can be calculated, but failure cannot be ruled out. Many investors use probability theory to calculate the likelihood of certain events happening. By contrast, speculation tends to be based not on deduction from facts but on half-truths and sheer rumour.

Probably the most famous speculative mania ever was the eighteenth-century South Sea Bubble. The South Sea Company was a London-based joint-stock company claiming to have monopoly rights to trade in Spanish America. It was so certain of success that in 1720 it offered to assume responsibility for the national debt in return for a guaranteed annual payment of five per cent. At the end of March, the House of Commons passed legislation in favour of this scheme with a massive majority. Robert Walpole, a former Chancellor of the Exchequer, who later became the first Prime Minister, spoke eloquently against the scheme—"the dangerous practice of stock-jobbing, [which] would divert the genius of the nation from trade and industry"—and then himself went on to speculate profitably in South Sea Company stock. Following the vote in Parliament, just as the canny South Sea Company directors must have anticipated, its share price rose dramatically—to £330, from around £128 in January at the beginning of the debate. Extravagant rumours now boosted confidence in the company and the share price rocketed. At the same time, ever more implausible speculative ventures were launched by others. A frenzy of buying by all and sundry, from noblemen to peasants, fuelled by borrowing, followed the initial rise, and pushed the South Sea Company share price up to £890 at the beginning

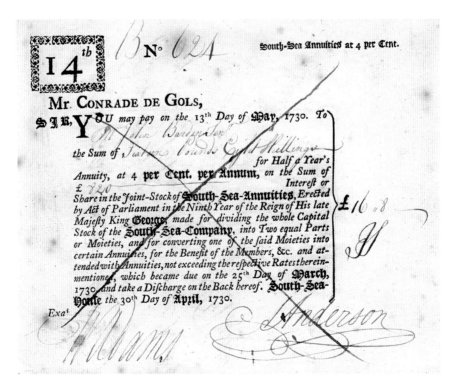

*Early certificate of the South Sea Company, which claimed to have monopoly rights to trade in Spanish America in the eighteenth century.*

of June, and even over £1000 in August. Then it began to fall, amidst rumours that some of the company's directors had sold out, and in September the price collapsed, crashing to £150 by the end of the month. The bubble burst when investors realized that the company's Spanish-American trading prospects were in harsh reality non-existent. Inevitably, many got out too late and were ruined, including members of the aristocracy—Walpole himself was saved only by the foresight of his banker Robert Jacomb.

Such speculative fever is probably part of human nature, and it hit the stock markets again in 2000 with the dotcom companies. Instead of assessing the internet companies' prospects, many investors simply threw their money at anything connected with dotcoms and suffered miserable returns as a result. They were encouraged in this, not only by the seductive promise of a new technology, but also by the unusually good performance of the stock market in the 1980s and 90s. Despite the major fall in October 1987, known as Black Monday, when Wall Street had its worst day of trading since 1914 and investors lost a quarter of their money, equities in these two decades gave a real return of 13.1 per cent, as compared with 5.7 per cent for most of the twentieth century. Indeed, during the period 1900–2003 shares produced negative returns in a third of the years, and some negative periods lasted for as long as ten years. Today, in a very fast-changing world, it has become increasingly difficult to predict the future performance of equities. This fact matters to everyone, not only the wealthy (as we shall see in chapter six). Although direct share ownership in Britain has actually fallen—from 54 per cent in 1963 to 20.5 per cent in 1997—as it has in the United States, ordinary people are heavily invested in equities through their endowment or life-insurance policies and their pension policies; it is estimated that between a half and two-thirds of pension money in Britain is invested in shares. In addition, governments—and hence taxpayers—depend on equity performance in servicing government debts.

Nonetheless, the consensus remains that, overall, capitalism is a force for public good, even though it is motivated by self-interest. Adam Smith's theory of the invisible hand is as potent now as it was in 1776, when he wrote *The Wealth of Nations*. Arguably, market forces are now more powerful than any government. Roger Backhouse writes in *The Penguin History of Economics* that, "The decisions people take in the market drive the economy towards greater efficiency, thanks to the combination of at least three common human desires: for a bargain, to do better and to get richer." That is certainly a fair description of what drove me into finance in the London of the mid-1950s, combined with my incipient excitement about the power of financial instruments, of the paper world. But first I had to research the markets and decide where to concentrate my attention. Was my choice to be the London money market, massive and long established, or would I perhaps do better overseas, where the chances of success seemed seriously tempting?

# CHAPTER 3

## Student of Finance: Dreams about Paper

*What is an investment? Putting money to work, in the hope of making more money. Investment takes two main forms: direct spending on buildings, machinery and so forth, and indirect spending on financial securities, such as bonds and shares.*

MATTHEW BISHOP, *Essential Economics*, 2004

My mother, who had moved to London in 1950 after separating from my father in Ceylon, was a dramatic, confident and hard-working person, who instilled tremendous confidence in her children too. Chelsea, the London borough where she, my sister and I lived after I left school, was in those days full of bohemians. But my mother told us that these other people were fakes—we Ondaatjes were the real bohemians! We certainly had no money to speak of—that was why I had had to leave school early—but what we did have was a belief in ourselves: that we were still aristocrats. When I was working at the National Bank of India (NBI) in the City, I believed I was some sort of a prince, despite my fairly menial position. I brimmed with confidence, and probably a certain amount of arrogance too. Those early years in the City were a terrific time for a young man just out of school, and I know that my mother worried, and with good reason, about how I might end up.

My confidence came not only from my mother and my family upbringing in Ceylon but also from the bank, which undoubtedly treated me very well. I played cricket and rugger for the bank's team and competed in athletics for the NBI, the Eastern Banks and the United

Banks. The bank was more than willing to give me time off to train and compete because it was good for their image; in fact the managers pampered me as a kind of star. Meanwhile, for nearly five years, they shifted me from department to department, so that I could learn the structure of the business before my probable move back to Ceylon to the bank's Colombo office. But really I had no clear purpose in life.

Then one day in 1954, while getting ready for the Institute of Bankers examination, I went to that eye-opening lecture at the London School of Economics. It was a gorgeous summer's evening when I should have been playing cricket, instead I was cooped up in a classroom. I expected a dull talk on economics—one of the five key subjects in the course— but what I heard changed my life. After a short introduction to the intricacies of economics, the lecturer went into a fundamental explanation of corporate finance and the things that constituted an 'investment': partnerships, limited liability, ordinary shares, shareholder rights, and so on and so forth. Because, I suppose, my mind was already primed by my practical exposure to finance at the NBI, the lecture came to me as a revelation. I decided then and there that if I were to have any sort of career at all, it would be in the world of paper finance. My fascination with the power of paper soon crystallized into a determination to be as independent as I could, and perhaps attempt to restore our lost family fortune.

But at the same time I was compelled to consider with ruthless realism whether Britain was really the right place for a lean and hungry 21-year-old 'colonial' from Ceylon, albeit someone partly educated at an English public school, to make his financial mark. The atmosphere of the City in the early 1950s, as I knew very well from my experience at the National Bank of India, was stuffy and cautious—old boy network and club culture in full force. Political and economic policies at the national level, even under the new Conservative government of 1951, were not conducive to entrepreneurs. Above all, Britain was obviously a declining world power, its Empire diminishing and its economy still in the toils of post-war austerity, suffering from the ravages of the Second World War, which had finished less than a decade earlier. I knew I had a tough and lonely decision ahead of me.

* * *

Britain had spent the 1940s in debt. The 1939–45 war cost the nation twice as much as the 1914–18 war and decimated the capacity of the export industries; about a quarter of the country's pre-war wealth was wiped out during the war years. By the time VE Day arrived in May 1945, Britain was overspending its income by more than £2000 million each year. During the war, the country had been sustained by Lend-Lease, an arrangement whereby the United States supplied military equipment and armaments, as well as food, to Britain and allied nations whose defence was considered vital to the defence of the United States— originally as a loan in return for the 'lease' of British-owned military bases. Lend-Lease propped up the British war effort from 1941 onwards, and the British government hoped it would continue during the transition period to a peacetime economy. Instead, the US government halted Lend-Lease immediately after the Japanese surrender in August 1945, leaving Britain floundering. Finance that had provided the country with about two-thirds of the funds needed to service a total external deficit of £10,000 million built up over the six years of war, was unilaterally withdrawn by the US without prior negotiation.

National pride had to be swallowed, and the new Prime Minister Clement Attlee sent John Maynard Keynes to Washington DC, begging bowl in hand. The terms of the loan he was offered were potentially devastating, however Britain had little choice but to accept. The Washington Loan Agreement secured Britain $3750 million, pushed up to $5000 million by a contribution from Canada. In return, the US government expected that within two years the pound sterling would be made fully convertible with the US dollar. But this did not go according to plan. The British winter of 1946–47 (just before I arrived in the country) was cruel—the worst of the century. Production suffered and coal shortages led to a drastic fuel crisis. Factories closed for three weeks, badly damaging the export drive. By the time convertibility was due to begin in 1947, the economy was too weak to bear it. Five weeks after convertibility came into effect, it had to be suspended because of a massive run on the pound, as holders of sterling tried to convert pounds into dollars. At the peak of the run, the outflow of gold and dollars reached $237 million in one week alone. It took yet another financial crisis, in 1949, during which the pound was devalued by about 30 per cent from $4.03 to $2.80, finally to rectify Britain's trade deficit with America.

The years of austerity from 1945–51 were ones of gradual, strained recovery under Labour. Food subsidies and rationing were retained to keep down living costs; progressive rates of taxation were kept in place; and regional development was vigorously pursued, helping to avoid any return to the mass unemployment of the 1930s in the pre-war industrial blackspots. A million new homes were built (80 per cent of them council owned) to provide dwellings for the growing population and those hit by bomb damage. The National Health Service (NHS) was launched (in 1948). All these economic policies designed to favour lower-income families slowly took effect.

However, further problems loomed due to Britain's overweening sense of its own importance in world affairs. The war might have brought the country to its knees, but after the bloody triumph of victory, as the only Western European nation successfully to have resisted Nazi invasion and occupation, still with the largest empire in the world, Britain continued to consider itself a major international power. During the war, Winston Churchill had provided and sustained the proud image of a Britain standing at the intersection of three overlapping circles: that of Europe, of the Empire and of the 'special relationship' with the US. After 1945, Labour's able foreign secretary Ernest Bevin maintained Britain's wartime view of itself, but as Peter Clarke points out in his history of Britain in the twentieth century, *Hope and Glory*, "Although his efforts were prodigious and his achievements considerable, they did not, of course, permanently reverse the trajectory of British decline. Indeed the question that seems obvious 50 years later is how much Britain was weakened by fighting above its weight."

The most obviously draining example of this attitude was Britain's involvement in the Korean War. Commitment to this far-off conflict necessitated a huge increase in defence spending. Attlee's planned defence programme would cost the country £4.7 billion over three years, well over ten per cent of the gross national product. It was Hugh Gaitskell, as Chancellor of the Exchequer for the April 1951 budget, who had to find the cash, which he did by bumping up taxes. The standard rate of income

*Clement Attlee's disastrous defence programme involving Britain in the Korean War would cost the nation £4.7 billion over three years— more than ten per cent of the gross national product.*

tax rose to 47.5 per cent and the top rate (including surtax) to 97.5 per cent. This was at the time I moved to London and first became a taxpayer myself. Gaitskell also intended to raise money by charging patients for dentures and spectacles provided by the NHS. His proposal precipitated a punishing political struggle within the Labour party between supporters of defence spending on rearmament and supporters of Aneurin Bevan (who had established the NHS) who held firm to the principle that the NHS should remain free at the point of use. The row led to Bevan's resignation and was a factor in the downfall of the Labour government in the 1951 election.

The burden of financing Britain's contribution in Korea then fell on the new Conservative Chancellor, Rab Butler, who was eventually forced to cut defence expenditure. But in the meantime, during the first half of the 1950s, the national income had improved significantly, up by 40 per cent in 1955 on the start of the decade. Butler was able to cut the standard rate of income tax to 42.5 per cent, the lowest rate since the end of the war, and a useful party-political move with an election set for 1955. Standards of living were now noticeably better: employment was still high, average weekly earnings had increased from £7 10s (£7.50) in 1950 to £11 in 1955—a rise of some 50 per cent over a period in which the cost of living rose by 30 per cent. As a result, the more affluent households could take advantage of the newly marketed washing machines, vacuum cleaners and other elbow-grease-saving appliances. A decent quality of life was becoming available, as the Conservative Prime Minister Harold Macmillan encapsulated a little later, in 1957, in a much-quoted speech: "Most of our people have never had it so good."

But while this was true, there was a downside. In 1954, it seemed to me that the changes brought in by the Attlee government, which had done so much to improve social welfare, had simultaneously generated a risk-averse culture that acted against personal enterprise, against creative business thinking, against taking the kind of risk that I would need to take if I were to succeed as I hoped.

The two world wars had demonstrated the potential benefits of greater state involvement in the economy. In line with the thinking of Keynes, and more particularly with the 1942 recommendations of the Beveridge Report (on Social Insurance and Allied Services), Labour's radical election pledge for Britain in 1945 involved a seismic shift in the management of social welfare and the economy. Government would become the partner and protector of the people: the state would take total responsibility for their welfare and education; full employment would be maintained; a number of important private enterprises would be taken into public ownership. The hope was, that by implementing this visionary programme, a 'New Jerusalem' would be established in which the suffering economy could recover from the blows of the war. The overall aim was protection for all 'from the cradle to the grave'.

After Labour's victory, Attlee's government set about fulfilling this program with a will. The National Insurance Act of 1946 greatly extended the existing sickness and unemployment schemes, making contributions compulsory for all and benefits almost universal. With regard to the state pension, Attlee exceeded William Beveridge's suggestions, providing pensions for women over 60 and men over 65 immediately, whereas Beveridge had called for a phased introduction, allowing for contributions to build up the national insurance fund. Such a commitment was costly to the taxpayer, but very popular among both the elderly and older workers. So too was the establishment of the National Health Service. Despite initial opposition from the Conservatives and the British Medical Association representing doctors—Bevan admitted he had resorted to "stuffing their mouths with gold" in order to overcome doctors' concerns about their loss of private income—the NHS is now widely seen as the crowning achievement of Attlee's government. The NHS undoubtedly enabled many in need of treatment to access a quality of medical care previously unavailable to them. Those who were not covered by these two Acts were provided for under the National Assistance Act of 1948, which abolished the feared and hated

Poor Laws that had been in place since Elizabethan times in the sixteenth century. The benefits of state welfare represented a dramatic advance in the social well-being of the working class.

Public ownership of business came swiftly under Labour. The Bank of England moved into the public domain in 1945. Coal mining was next in 1947, gas was nationalized in 1948, with electricity and the railways to follow. Peter Clarke argues that, "In all of these examples, a strong pragmatic case existed, in line with classical principles of free competition, for eliminating private monopoly by taking essential utilities into public ownership. This was not, however, the case which appealed to socialists, who preferred to dwell on the abolition of the capitalist system through dispossession of the tsars of big business."

In his right-wing critique of the period, *The Audit of War: The Illusion and Reality of Britain as a Great Nation*, published in 1986, Correlli Barnett blamed the prevalence of 'New Jerusalem' thinking for Britain's post-war industrial decline, claiming that it "tipped the whole balance of Whitehall's collective attention towards desirable social goals rather than industrial performance". According to Barnett's argument, the welfare state was a costly burden and Labour's prioritization of welfare reform over economic realism caused the country to fail to rebuild industrially at the point when its international rivals offered relatively weak competition. However, few other academic historians have agreed with Barnett, who was, unsurprisingly, a useful figure for Conservatives under Margaret Thatcher who wished to reduce the role of the state in the 1980s.

One might have expected the Conservative victory in 1951 (which occurred shortly after I started at the National Bank of India) to have put some of the radical Labour policies into reverse. But in practice this did not occur. While the new government may have wanted as little direct intervention in the economy as possible, Britain's involvement in the Korean War required economic controls to be maintained and only gradually abandoned. The later Conservative commitment to creating an 'opportunity' state, rather than a 'welfare' state, to tax cuts and to the explicit promotion of economic growth as a key objective—all of which happened in the late 1950s—arrived too late for me.

As for the trade with the Empire, on which my bank relied so heavily, this started, very gradually at first, to crumble in the early 1950s. Some historians have plausibly seen the decline in Britain's economic influence as the primary cause of imperial dissolution, particularly in those formally self-governing areas, such as Canada, where Britain's power relied on commercial predominance rather than constitutional ties. Until the Second World War, the dominions, the dependencies and the semi-colonial regions had relied on British markets for their exports, had used London's banks to handle their international trade, and had depended upon British manufactures. But during and after the war, Britain had sustained itself by running up massive debts to the Empire in the form of sterling balances. A billion pounds was owed to India alone, with another £400 million to Egypt and Sudan. The Empire also played a crucial role in reasserting the equilibrium between the dollar and sterling areas after convertibility was introduced; borrowing from the Empire was a useful alternative to even more punitive domestic austerity or taking further loans from the US. Having once been the greatest creditor of its Empire, by the early 1950s Britain had become its poorest debtor.

In his *Britain and Decolonisation: The Retreat from Empire in the Post-war World*, John Darwin writes about this change: "While Britain remained the world's greatest source of development capital, the principal centre of international finance and the largest market for primary products, the possibility of the colonies achieving real, as opposed to merely constitutional, independence from the mother country remained somewhat limited." But if Britain could not sustain this role, adds Darwin, "it could only be a matter of time before the Empire countries who were free to do so looked elsewhere for economic partners and financial patrons, while the unfree dependencies rebelled against a colonial system that offered no economic benefits. Nor, indeed, without her old financial strength would Britain long have the power to enforce her control of the dependencies."

Still, despite Britain's weakness, for a while ties remained close. The dominions were willing to accept the controls upon their economies that Britain imposed and desperately needed, partly out of loyalty engendered by the shared experience of war and partly for a more pragmatic reason—while Britain remained their banker, the dominions had an interest in preventing the bank's financial collapse. When sterling-dollar convertibility was introduced in 1947 as a result of the Washington Loan Agreement, the dominions were once again free to exchange exports for non-sterling goods—a great benefit—but they were relatively acquiescent when Britain hastily put a stop to this. They also agreed to make withdrawals from their now-substantial sterling reserves in London at a rate slow enough not to pressure the British economy too strongly. In this way, the Empire helped Britain narrowly to evade the "financial Dunkirk" that Keynes had predicted in 1945.

For all Britain's pretensions to international importance, the realities of the post-war world put the country firmly in its place as an American satellite. The United States had been the power that had gained most economically from the war. Between 1940 and 1944, industrial output in the US grew by 15 per cent each year. At the end of the conflict, the US owned two thirds of the world's gold bullion, half of its supply of shipping and supplied a third of its exports. Britain's financial dependence on the US inevitably had some influence on decisions about the Empire. In August 1941, Churchill and Roosevelt had signed the Atlantic Charter promising to uphold "the rights of all peoples to choose the form of government under which they live" and "to see sovereign rights of self-government restored to those who have been forcibly deprived of them". Churchill assumed that much of the Empire would be exempt from the charter, but American opinion was virulently anti-imperialist. At an emotional level, empire of any kind was thought to be tyrannous and oppressive. In 1942–45, it was mostly American soldiers who were fighting in the Pacific, and there was considerable discontent among them that their victories and their loss of life were making it possible for Britain to hold on to colonies such as Burma and Malaya, so as to maintain its morally questionable Empire. In addition, the US government regarded the long-term continuation of the sterling area as a hindrance to the opening up of international trade and free markets.

With the benefit of hindsight and history books, it is easy to assume that the combination of Britain's devastated economy, American pressure and increasingly vigorous nationalist movements in the colonies should have shown Britain that it could not keep hold of its Empire for much longer. But most British politicians of both left and right did not draw this conclusion—rather the opposite. My experience of banking in London, from 1951–56, fell between two distinct phases in the dismantling of the Empire. During the first phase, in 1947–48, India and the rest of South Asia had gone—but this region was considered to be an exception to the rest of the Empire, since Indian independence had been talked about for quite a while because of the country's deep-rooted and organized nationalist movement, and even before the Second World War India had made significant progress towards self-government. So India's departure was not widely regarded as the beginning of the end of Empire. Then, ten years later, after a lengthy period of eloquent and sometimes violent anti-colonial nationalism and a sharp diminution of imperial ambition in Britain, the second phase began, with the independence of Ghana in 1957. Between the two phases, however, in the late 1940s and early 1950s, most British politicians remained committed to retaining the rest of the Empire while using the Commonwealth of Nations (as the British Commonwealth of Nations inaugurated in 1931 was renamed in 1946) to preserve British interests, both strategic and economic.

My homeland Ceylon had, of course, been part of the first phase of decolonization. The transfer of power in Ceylon was unusually smooth, especially when compared with the violent mess in Burma (which did not join the Commonwealth) and the bloodletting of the India/Pakistan partition. Ceylon became a dominion in February 1948 under the leadership of D. S. Senanayake, the head of the United Nationalist Party, and immediately joined the Commonwealth. Two agreements setting out Anglo-Ceylonese cooperation in defence and external affairs were signed. Such a willingness to remain closely allied with the British may have been a consequence of the Sinhalese majority's fears of their possible future domination by India. Certainly, most of Ceylon's politicians seemed content with the new situation: they were "extremely friendly and want to maintain and deepen the British connection," wrote the British junior minister Patrick Gordon-Walker in 1948. Trade, especially in tea, continued to be a strong tie, and the hope was that trade would continue to flourish while the Commonwealth provided a psychological cushion to soften the blow of the severance of the South Asian part of the Empire.

In the meantime, the government in London believed that the remaining colonies could play a vital role in restoring British power and influence. They had helped Britain survive six years of terrible conflict, now they could boost the mother country through her peacetime economic problems. The British Treasury saw the tremendous possibilities of colonial exports for earning dollars. Malayan rubber and Gold Coast cocoa already had large US markets, which could be further exploited; Malayan tin and rubber earned more US dollars in 1948 than the total exports of Britain. Foreign Secretary Bevin declared: "We have the material resources in the Colonial empire, if we develop them, and by giving a spiritual lead now we should be able to carry out our task in a way which will show clearly that we are not subservient to the United States of America or the Soviet Union." Indeed, Bevin went much further than envisaging British equality with these two great powers: "If we only pushed and developed Africa, we could have the US dependent on us, eating out of our hands in four or five years."

Belief in the potential of colonial development created a number of new projects, including the notorious East African groundnuts scheme of 1946. The plan looked like it would be a winner: the mass cultivation of groundnuts in Tanganyika, and from them the production of margarine and cooking oils, would add much-needed calories to the meagre diet in Britain, where rationing was causing increased discontent, while also providing much-needed cash for purchasing imports. But the reality was a disaster—soil erosion made much of the land unsuitable for mechanized cultivation and unforeseen plant viruses destroyed the crops—and after £30 million had been invested, the project was abandoned in the early 1950s. This embarrassing flop has come to symbolize a more general failure of colonial development, but it nevertheless demonstrates the Labour government's continuing faith in the Empire not only to shore up Britain's international status but also to support and subsidize the domestic standard of living. To quote Bevin once more, speaking in the House of Commons in February 1946, "I am not prepared to sacrifice the British Empire because I know that if the British Empire fell . . . it would mean the standard of living of our constituents would fall considerably." Between 1945 and 1954, staffing numbers at the Colonial Office grew by 43 per cent—yet more evidence of the British government's commitment to a potentially bountiful empire.

The idea of the Commonwealth countries and the colonies acting as Britain's economic saviour was not inherently unrealistic—in 1950, for the first time, over half of British exports went to these markets—but it was a creature of the particular, and peculiar, circumstances of the immediate aftermath of the war. The economic recovery in trade with the Empire occurred at a time when British domestic consumption was being squeezed through high taxes and rationing and when the damage suffered by Western Europe and Japan made those countries uncompetitive in export markets. This was a situation that could not last long. From 1948, generous American aid to Western Europe under the Marshall Plan enabled these countries to rebuild relatively rapidly, while the Commonwealth and colonial markets expanded more slowly. After 1950, British manufacturers had real competition; gone were the days of scarcity during and immediately after the war when companies made good profits from selling almost anything they could make. In 1950, the British command of world manufactures was 25 per cent, but by 1970, it was down to 10 per cent. Trade with the colonies was affected, too: British exports to colonial markets decreased from 29 per cent to 23 per cent in the period 1953–58, while imports from the same source dropped from 31 per cent to 23 per cent. "As the world moved out of the economics of siege and into a freer economic order, Britain's claims to the economic and 'natural' leadership of the Commonwealth-Sterling area would once again come to depend upon her own industrial strength, commercial enterprise and capital resources," comments Darwin.

Britain's trade relationship with India, although it took a decade and more to deteriorate, is a good example of how imperial economics changed. At the time of Indian independence in 1947, the prospects for a lasting and mutually rewarding relationship between Britain and its ex-colony looked excellent. India had deep reserves of sterling with which to purchase British goods and the country remained attractive in terms of profits on sales and returns on investment, to exporters and investors. At the same time, firms with close ties to London dominated India's international trading and banking systems. Between 1948 and mid-1956, commercial links were almost as secure as in the colonial era. But then there was a decline, which accelerated in the 1960s. British industry's increasing lack of competitiveness and the depletion of Indian sterling balances meant that India turned towards other potential trading partners. "In 1970, British exports to India were worth half as much as in 1960, and one-third of the real 1956 level," note Michael Lipton and John Firn in *The Erosion of a Relationship: India and Britain since 1960*. British domination of the Indian market was replaced by American and Soviet influence, as India steadily disengaged from her reliance on British suppliers and markets.

During my time at the National Bank of India, the erosion had barely started. Colonial and Commonwealth business at the bank was pretty healthy, and my colleagues and superiors were content. But to me it seemed increasingly clear that the colonies could not provide a cure-all for deep-rooted problems of British uncompetitiveness. I felt sure that many colonies and dominions would have more to gain from non-imperial than from imperial trade. And that the freer they were from old British political ties, the freer they would be to seek out more lucrative economic arrangements.

Analyzing the various reasons for decolonization and weighing up historical economic statistics can only be a retrospective activity. Back in 1954, looking around me in the City and at the country as a whole, I convinced myself that the future would not include the successful continuation of the British Empire and that the financial benefits of that empire would therefore disappear. I am still proud of this glimmer of historical foresight at a time when it was not in common currency. By 1956, and the national embarrassment of the Suez crisis—the event that really signalled the end of the Empire—my ticket out of the country was booked.

In 1954, after passing the Institute of Bankers examination, my plan for the next few years was to emigrate and learn everything I could about finance and the instruments of finance. I would research the markets and their rates of return, study the entrepreneurs who had succeeded before me, learn about the players in my chosen field and weigh up potential rewards and risks. Then, only then, would be the time to start my own business. Without any personal money, I knew I had to start small, but it never occurred to me I might fail. Looking back, such unhesitating self-belief seems outrageously presumptuous—but at the time I never questioned my optimism.

So where best to try my luck? The most obvious choice for anyone dreaming of riches in the twentieth century had to be the United States, and it was America that I considered first. The US, after all, was the first country fully to embrace the limited-liability company and the paper financing of unfettered free enterprise during the nineteenth century.

From the creation of the greenback in 1862 to the seven trillion dollars circulating in today's world (albeit most of them in electronic form), the US financial system has come to dominate global business. In the twentieth century, the dollar became much more than a simple medium of exchange; it was fraught with symbolic and psychological significance. It stood for America's sense of purpose and the promise of the New World, setting Federalists against Republicans, farmers against gold-diggers, and the power of democracy against the money power of Wall Street. If the business of America is business, then the dollar is America's icon.

My guides to American economic history were two books now considered classics of their kind: *The Age of the Moguls*, Stewart Holbrook's breathless account of the businesses and businessmen who built the United States, which was published in London in 1954, and Matthew Josephson's biographical account of the great American capitalists of the late nineteenth century, *The Robber Barons*. As its title suggests, Josephson's book, which appeared during the great depression of the 1930s, is less awestruck than Holbrook's by the men who developed a half-empty continent, brought about the US industrial revolution and amassed vast personal wealth in the process. But both books are written in a purple, rousing prose that suits their larger-than-life subjects and appealed very much, I freely admit, to my youthful imagination and ambitions. I devoured the books' stories of progress from obscurity to riches by such buccaneering figures as Andrew Carnegie, John D. Rockefeller and Cornelius Vanderbilt. The two authors may not have liked their protagonists much, but they could not hide their admiration for them, and this tension made for a fascinating read. "The men in this book have been variously described during a century as giants and Titans, and more often as rogues, robbers and rascals. But never as feeble. The least of them had a splendid audacity and a vital energy that erupted in astonishing ways," enthuses Holbrook, while Josephson exclaims more succinctly: "How much panache those old barons had!"

*The Age of the Moguls* details not only the flamboyant figures, it also

*In the early 1950s, my guides to American business history were two books, now considered classics of their kind: Stewart Holbrook's* The Age of the Moguls *and Matthew Josephson's* The Robber Barons.

tells the stories of incredibly wealthy but unassuming men. For example, Andrew Mellon, born in Pittsburgh in 1855. The son of a banker, Mellon grew the family business beyond anything imaginable by his father. But despite this success, Mellon was both shy and invisible to the public as a financier. Unlike Henry Ford, an industrial boss known to thousands of his workers, Mellon was known to only a few hundred men in a handful of corporations and, outside of Pittsburgh, hardly at all.

It was in 1880 that Mellon took control of his father's bank only ten years after its foundation. Unlike other banks, the Mellon bank was known for its probity and for its efforts to fund worthwhile enterprises. The Mellons located honest, capable entrepreneurs who needed capital. If a new business passed the Mellons' stringent investigation, funds were forthcoming and so long as the business was well managed the bank left it alone. After the business became a going concern and the loan was repaid, the Mellons used the profit to fund another enterprise in need of capital. Andrew Mellon's most astute investment was in the Pittsburgh Reduction Company (later the Aluminum Company of America), a young business which had devised a method for smelting aluminium. Two highly regarded capitalists had already rejected the company as an investment but Mellon was impressed by the sample pieces of metal he saw and decided to advance the required capital in exchange for sufficient stock to control the company, while allowing Charles Hall, the inventor of the process, to own a third of the total stock. Both Mellon and Hall went on to make a mint out of aluminium. The uses of the metal proliferated—from soldiers' kits to radiators and later to mass-produced automobiles. Mellon protected his position by using patent law to win a legal battle against another aluminium manufacturer in a settlement said to have been worth $100 million to the Mellon family.

Everyone had now heard of aluminium but few knew of Andrew Mellon, until he entered the political world and became Secretary of the Treasury in 1921. During his decade in office, one of his fiscal reforms became known to all Americans and remains a familiar fact of life around the world even today: the size of US banknotes. The new notes introduced at the behest of Mellon were only two thirds the size of the bills that had been used for decades. According to one of his biographers, Philip Love, the smaller format saved the government "$552,520 on paper, $120,000 in ink, and a round million dollars in labour". Thus Mellon's careful use of paper, even when he was no longer acting as a great financier, was still highly productive.

As well as the personalities, these two business books introduced me to Wall Street and the American way of financial thinking. I could not help my admiration for the legendary financier J. P. Morgan. In the 1880s and 1890s, when rampant capitalism threatened to spiral out of control in the US, Morgan created a virtual economic command centre based on his far-flung financial interests in the railway, shipping, coal, insurance and communications industries. "No other of the great money-lords had so purposeful a mind and so resolute a program" (*The Robber Barons*). The order Morgan imposed on the whole economy gave it a coherence and direction it would otherwise have lacked. Morgan continued to be the country's foremost financier until his death in 1913, by which time he had given away substantial portions of his wealth to charities, churches, hospitals and schools. Much of his huge collection of art went to The Metropolitan Museum of Art in New York.

Reading about Morgan and the other moguls, my reaction was not simply passive wonder at their achievements (combined with raised eyebrows at their sometimes dubious business methods and their eccentricities). At the same time, I thought, broadly speaking, "I could do that!" However, I was keenly aware that the United States of the 1950s was not the United States of the post-Civil War era, "a paradise for the entrepreneur, untrammelled and untaxed", to quote Josephson again. In Morgan's or indeed Mellon's day, the opportunity for the private banker was almost limitless in a country "whose population doubles in two decades, whose industrial construction must be extended almost incessantly, whose underground resources demand ever larger exploitation." By the mid-1950s, although the US was evidently rich, powerful and still growing, I felt that opportunities for a newcomer, particularly opportunities to experiment or diversify, were becoming scarcer. And Wall Street was not a place where mistakes would go unnoticed. In short, enthralled though I was by US capitalism, the United States intimidated me.

Having decided against the USA, I looked momentarily at far-off Australia. Its warm climate, relative proximity to Ceylon and love of cricket were tempting factors, but somehow my brief investigations into the continent did not fire my enthusiasm, and I turned restlessly back to the atlas once again. This time I let my gaze wander north, up the coastline of America to consider a country about which I knew almost nothing—Canada.

Canada has always had a mixed press beyond Canada. Perceptions of its opportunities and possibilities have varied wildly throughout its history. Many have dismissed the second largest country in the world as an irrelevant appendix to its more powerful, attention-seeking southerly neighbour. "Canada?" asked Chicago's Al Capone (so they say), "I don't even know what street Canada is on." The famous *New Yorker* 'map' of the world as seen from New York (drawn by Saul Steinberg) shows Canada as a puny triangle of land poking in from the right-hand edge next to Chicago.

Obviously geography has a lot to do with this image of insignificance. Much of Canada indisputably does consist of icy wilderness. When the explorer Jacques Cartier—who is sometimes given credit for naming Canada by mistaking the Mohawk word for village (*kana:ta'*) for the name of the whole land—arrived on the south coast of Labrador in the 1530s, he declared: "In all the north land I did not see a cartload of good earth. To be short, I believe that this was the land that God allotted to Cain." In 1866, a travel writer in *Lippincott's Gazetteer* foresaw a gloomy future for the country: "There can be but little doubt that the greater part of the vast region included under the name of British America is doomed to everlasting sterility on account of the severity of its climate." To this day the polar regions of Canada—the Yukon territory, the Northwest territories and Nunavut—make up over 41 per cent of the land mass but contain only 0.3 per cent of the population. The great majority of Canadians live in a narrow strip of land within 200 miles of the United States; the inhabitants of Canada's three biggest cities can drive across the US-Canada border in under two hours.

Along with the supposed insignificance of the country goes a reputation for lack of dynamism, a polite torpor, epitomized in a recent internet discussion of Canada by one contributor who called it "the Clark Kent of countries, but without the Superman alter ego". But others have strongly disagreed with this view. Particularly during the twentieth century, Canada has been seen as a resource-rich land of plenty and potential. Its abundance of minerals and raw materials, its relative openness to immigrants, and its people's reputation for calm and culture have led it to be held in high esteem. Churchill considered that, "There are no limits to the majestic future which lies before the mighty expanse of Canada with its virile, aspiring, cultured, and generous-hearted people," and John Maynard Keynes declared that Canada was his country of choice should he ever leave Britain. "Canada is a place of infinite promise," wrote Keynes during the Second World War.

Such heavyweight endorsements—and there were others—influenced me in London in the mid-1950s. Though I had no links with the country, it was only natural to investigate Canada as a potential stage for my business plans. I needed to consider more closely what Canada had to offer a newcomer without money. How open really was the country to immigrant adventurers? What recent precedents were there for the success of new enterprises? How did its post-war economic climate compare with Britain's?

A little reading revealed that modern Canada had its roots in trade and enterprise. The earliest European settlements, in the fifteenth and sixteenth centuries, were on the coast of Newfoundland and Nova Scotia, made by English and French fishermen drying out their catches in the summer months before the long sail home. Eventually, some settlements became permanent. The fur trade, partly through the Hudson's Bay Company, was responsible for helping to populate the vast Canadian interior, as Europeans traded guns, textiles and luxury items for pelts (mostly beaver) trapped by the indigenous Canadians. Rivalry between the English and the French was present from the beginning, and it increased during the eighteenth century as the British gradually seized the French Canadian possessions—first Acadia (Nova Scotia), then Quebec, until in 1759 all of New France was conquered. In the nineteenth century, timber became the largest export and played an important role in attracting and retaining immigrants; at the peak of the trade in the 1840s, there were 15,000 Irish loggers in the Gatineau region alone (as compared to a mere 10,000 people in Montreal a few years before this). When logging declined in the second half of the century, the pulp and paper industry became central to Canadian exports. Near the end of the century and after, there was a mining boom, especially for gold, silver, copper and, in the 1930s, uranium. (Canada's uranium was later vital in making the wartime atomic bombs.) Indeed, between 1896 and 1914, technological and agricultural development made Canada the world's fastest-growing economy, provoking Prime Minister Wilfrid Laurier to predict in 1900 that the twentieth century would belong to Canada.

This superficial reading piqued my interest. Here was a country built by adventurers and immigrants, with a strong frontier spirit. I was intrigued by the enduring French influence, which led me to hope that Canada might be a more ethnically diverse, open society than the Britain of the 1950s. But what of the country's recent past? Would the outlook for a young businessman really be rosier in the alien freezing climes of Canada than in the rainy old England I had come to know?

Canada had had a good war economically speaking; it was the war that finally pulled the country out of a long and brutal period of depression in the 1930s. During the war, Canada made a remarkable economic contribution to the Allied cause, with the major share of its arms production going to its allies and with much of that output financed by Canada through a combination of debt repayment, grants, loans, 'mutual aid', and other forms of assistance. Canadian factories were dedicated to building tanks, guns, ships and aircraft, notably fighter planes and Lancaster bombers. War production had been guided by C. D. Howe, the federal Minister of Munitions and Supply, who imposed a system of central planning, with wage and price controls. Many advances in technologies and engineering techniques were made and so the country entered the post-war era with a manufacturing capacity much more diverse than in 1939. The $1250 million loan that Canada offered Britain after the end of Lend-Lease in 1945, was a much larger commitment than the $3750 million offered by the United States in the

*Canada made a remarkable economic contribution to the Allied cause in the Second World War, guided in great part by C. D. Howe, the federal Minister of Munitions and Supply.*

Washington Loan Agreement, as a proportion of the country's gross national product. It was proof of Canada's wartime wealth and also a testament to the Canadian government's belief in the importance of international trade in nurturing European reconstruction and prosperity.

However, the transition to a peacetime economy still had to be managed carefully. As in Britain under Labour, at the end of the war, there was considerable Canadian support for increased state involvement in the economy. The success of the wartime command economy and pressure from the socialist party, the popular Cooperative Commonwealth Foundation (CCF), led many—businessmen included—

to push for greater governmental control of industry and for protection from the risks of the old free-market system. In fact, the first government formed by the CCF, the provincial government of Saskatchewan elected in 1944, pioneered Medicare, the system of universal government-funded medical insurance, which was much later introduced nationwide.

Under Mackenzie King's leadership during and after the war until 1948, the Canadian government reached a new high of intervention in the economy. It initiated national unemployment insurance, loans to small business and increased aid for housing, as well as offering support to the unions' drive for collective bargaining. However, there was less support for all this than in Britain, because Canada was not attempting to rebuild a war-ravaged economy. Businessmen soon declared some anxiety about the prospect of state planning squeezing private enterprise and began to resist further government involvement in industry. The public too, although it wanted more social security, also desired material prosperity and the new consumer goods—freezers, cars, nylons and furniture, not to speak of new houses in the suburbs—which were being accumulated by their American neighbours across the border.

The concerns of the business world tallied with those of the influential Howe, who became Minister of Reconstruction in 1944 when it became clear that the war would be won by the Allies. Until then, Howe had largely supported government control of industry as essential for the war effort, but he now moved away from this position. Michael Bliss explains in a chapter of his economic history of Canada, *Northern Business*, entitled (with an ironic nod to Adam Smith) "Visible hand: the years of C. D. Howe", that: "Howe . . . opposed some of the most ambitious government spending and control programs . . . He wanted rapid decontrol rather than continued planning—there would be no five-year plans or grand industrial strategies in Howe's Canada—and moved quickly to dismantle much of the government's business apparatus." The Canadian government's post-war dismantling of controls might have been slower and more measured than in the US, but it went much faster than in post-war Britain. As early as 1944, Howe granted accelerated depreciation to companies converting their business to peacetime production, which allowed them a swift write-off of extra expenses against current taxation. His overall intention was that post-war Canada would be a free-enterprise society.

The economic growth that began in the 1940s accelerated in the 1950s and, instead of the feared post-war depression, Canada boomed as the pent-up consumer demand from the war and the pre-war depression triggered what would turn out to be decades of sustained economic growth. There were fortunes to be made in retailing, real estate and construction. Between 1952 and 1957, new investment increased by 66 per cent, or 249 per cent since 1944. But it was industrial growth and a boom in resources that contributed most to Canada's blossoming; a world laid low by war had a vital need for Canada's abundant raw materials, while the discovery of oil in Alberta gradually made that province one of the country's richest. At the same time, Canadian-American economic integration grew stronger and cross-border trade increased; US natural resources were no longer sufficient on their own to satisfy the growing American military and industrial requirements (a demand fuelled further by the start of the Korean War in 1950). As a result, more and more US investment funds flowed into its northern neighbour's pockets. By the end of the twentieth century, Canada had finally thrown off its colonial yoke, as the US, rather than Britain, became its major investor.

New prosperity and optimism produced a spurt in population. Between 1946 and 1961, the population grew by 50 per cent, from 12 to 18 million. This was partly a result of a baby boom, an increase in the Canadian birth rate, which was one of the highest of any industrialized nation by the late 1950s. (It peaked in 1959, when there was a more than one in five chance of a woman in her twenties giving birth that year.) But there were also rising numbers of immigrants, which went up from 12,000 in 1944 to 125,000 in 1948. By 1950, the demand for immigrants exceeded supply, and the government made provision by widening the admissible classes of European immigrant. This change maintained the preference for British, Irish, French and American immigrants, who were all believed to be suited to the climatic, educational, social, industrial and labour environment of Canada. In practice, it meant many Canadian residents (excluding Asians) could sponsor relatives. A variety of semi-skilled and skilled immigrants, including domestics, agriculturalists, entrepreneurs and professionals, and any other worker sponsored by a Canadian employer, could now enter Canada. In the peak post-war year, 1957, 282,000 immigrants arrived—37,000 of them Hungarian refugees fleeing from Soviet repression of the Hungarian uprising the previous year. The Liberal Canadian government provided free transportation to these refugees by air and by sea, and the federal and provincial governments cooperated in making special arrangements to provide financial and medical assistance for them. No doubt most of these Hungarians settled in the cities, as was increasingly the demographic picture across Canada: during the years 1951–56, the proportion of urban dwellers rose by ten per cent so that it embraced two-thirds of all Canadians (the previous ten per cent increase had taken 40 years).

Many of Canada's twentieth-century immigrants had done well, like their predecessors. Some of them had helped to transform Canada's economy during the first half of the century, like their American counterparts—there were Canadian equivalents as wily, determined and diverse as Carnegie, Rockefeller and Morgan (as we shall shortly see). And nearly all had started from nothing. One of them, Stephen Roman, a Slovak immigrant to Canada in 1937 who started as a tomato picker, drifted into ethnic editing and then got into mining promotion, ended up running Consolidated Denison Mines, which in 1957 had more reserves of uranium ore than the entire United States. Admittedly, mining uranium had not a lot to do with my preferred world of paper, but Roman's was still an encouraging story of success. (Much later, in

*Stephen Roman, a Slovak immigrant to Canada in 1937, started as a tomato picker and ended up running Consolidated Denison Mines, which in 1957 had more reserves of uranium ore than the entire United States.*

1967, Roman's commercial interest in my first book, *The Prime Ministers of Canada*, would help me to get started in book publishing, as described in chapter five.)

All in all, Canada in 1956 looked welcoming for an entrepreneur without money and connections. It seemed like a country still discovering its own potential, growing and progressing in a way that the Britain I knew was not. Over the past 60 years, Britain has shifted from a near-command economy in 1945 to one of the least regulated economies in Western Europe. Britain has more in common now, in terms of its links between business, government and trade unions, with the United States, than with many of its neighbours in the European Union. Were

I starting out today, wondering where in the world would prove the most fertile ground for my twenty-something self to realize his paper dreams, I might elect to stay in London. But 50 years ago, I decided to get on a boat for Canada and see where it would lead me.

# CHAPTER 4

# *Investing in Canada: A New World of Paper*

*Canada is a place of infinite promise. We like the people, and if one ever had to emigrate, this would be the destination, not the USA. The hills, lakes and forests make it a place of peace and repose of the mind, such as one never finds in the USA.*

JOHN MAYNARD KEYNES, in a letter to his sister, 1944

I am not usually frightened to cut and run, or to be alone, or to take a gamble. I had some experience of all these things in Ceylon and England, through my tea plantation childhood, my parents' divorce and my disrupted schooling, In Canada, all of them would be a refrain throughout my business career—including the ultimate moment when I decided to sell everything and leave the financial world for ever. Even so, arrival in Canada was a shock. From being a rising star in a London bank, I had fallen to earth with a rude thud. Hardly anybody I now met was interested in my cricket or rugger or my English accent. But I did have an incredible sense of freedom. I told myself: "You're really on your own now!"

When I reached Toronto, I had thirteen Canadian dollars in my pocket—no other money. I did not have any help from my family, and promised myself never to write home for money; anyway, neither of my parents had any cash to spare. I also had one contact, a Canadian whom I had met in London, who played the trumpet and was part of a jazz group. Mike White eventually became well known in Toronto as the leader of the Imperial Jazz Band, which played in the Colonial Tavern on Yonge Street, the best nightclub in Canada. But when I got in touch with him, Mike was almost out of money too. However, he had a rented basement apartment for me in Leaside. My rent was $10 a week (in advance). I would pay him back later. The room I got was really the landlord's laundry room, so I slept surrounded by wet sheets. For food, I survived on ten-cent slices of toast from a local diner spread with free ketchup or mayonnaise, and sometimes raided the upstairs refrigerator for milk, watering the remainder. I had to get a job—fast.

Penniless, with my confidence severely dented though not completely squashed, I went to a government employment office and stood in a long line-up. There were a large number of Italian immigrants waiting, mostly looking for work in the construction industry, and I expected to be given some kind of rough labour, like digging ditches in the frozen north. But I was fortunate; my experience in a bank counted for something. When I reached the front of the line and talked to a clerk, he offered me a job in the cage at Burns Brothers and Denton, a stockbroking firm. Although I had no idea what a 'cage' was, I immediately accepted. Here was an entrée into the financial world, however low, and I was elated.

As I quickly learnt, in Canada the cage was the name for the administrative and accounting area where client trades were processed, settled and recorded. It was nowhere close to the main action on the trading floor. Certainly, I was dealing constantly with paper trades, as thousands of bonds and shares were bought and sold, but not quite in the way I had envisaged. Instead of controlling the paper myself, I was pushing it back and forth for others—over and over again. I could watch fortunes being made by them, especially in mining with companies like Rio Tinto and Noranda Mines, in front of my very eyes. I felt like a boy with no pocket money gazing into the window of a wonderful candy shop. But at the same time, I knew that the bundles of share certificates passing through my hands day after day were teaching me useful, up-to-date, hard information about contemporary Canada and modern Canadian business that I needed—and very much desired—to understand.

*     *     *

The fact most obvious from all this trading was that the Canadian economy was expanding fast. It actually trebled in size between 1945 and 1957, and the average weekly wage of factory workers doubled in the same period. Hence the population increase—in 1956, the population of Canada stood at 16 million, up by a third on the population ten years earlier, at the end of the war.

Hardly less obvious was that much of this growth was driven by investment coming from across the border. Some of the reasons for this American money flooding into Canada were mentioned in chapter three. But it is worth going into the Canada-United States relationship a bit more deeply, since it was becoming more and more important in the 1950s and would later influence my own business.

For most of its history, Canada had been almost exclusively a supplier of agricultural products and unfinished raw materials to the industrialized countries of the world. Then in 1939, the outbreak of the Second World War shook the Canadian economy to its core, because its usual export markets in Europe suddenly disappeared. In addition, its supply of manufactured goods from Britain and the rest of Europe was cut off. So when the United States entered the war at the end of 1941, American military spending came as a huge relief and boon to Canada, transforming its economy in a period of only three or four years. Arms production was like a protective tariff wall around the country, since normal business competition ceased. The war fostered rapid industrial growth and the introduction of new technologies, as mentioned earlier. By the end of it, in 1945, when the infrastructure of a large part of continental Europe lay in ruins and Britain was virtually bankrupt, Canada had acquired a greatly expanded industrial base. Agriculture and raw materials were still crucial to its economy but manufacturing was now important (by 1950, manufacturing accounted for fully half of the total value of Canada's production). As a direct result of the war, the country had the second highest standard of living in the world after the US.

After the war, Britain and Europe needed Canada's natural resources again, but they were destitute. As we know, Canada tried to help by extending credit to the devastated European economies and accepting sterling from Britain so as to keep trade going, but this situation could not continue indefinitely. At the same time, Canadians went on a post-war binge, spending on consumer goods, many of which were manufactured in the United States. But Americans would not accept Canadian trade credits or payment in sterling. Canada was caught in a bind: it could not convert the European demand for its raw materials into American dollars to pay for its own demand for US goods. The result was a currency crisis.

It was clear to many Canadians, though not all, that the country needed a free trade agreement with the US. The most powerful minister in the Mackenzie King government during and after the war, C. D. Howe, who was a naturalized Canadian born in the US, had good contacts in Washington DC. During the height of the war, as Minister of Munitions and Supply, Howe had ensured that Canadian and American diplomats and senior civil servants worked closely together, and consequently there was admiration in Washington for the competence of Canadian government servants. Howe also had an abiding faith in Canada's ability to compete globally, which would require Canada to have unrestricted access to American markets so as to achieve the necessary economies of scale. In this he was supported by skilful senior negotiators from the Department of Finance who thought that joining economic forces with the US would solve the currency crisis. A free-trade agreement with the US was therefore drafted in the spring of 1948. But later in that year it was killed off by the Prime Minister, King, who was on the verge of retirement and was worried that free trade would be seen as a sell-out to America and a cold shoulder to Britain. King knew that the Canadian public still felt strong ties to the mother country, and neither the public nor the government as a whole were keen to be locked into the economic orbit of the US. Nonetheless, despite the failure of a free-trade agreement, Canada secured many trade benefits with its partners in Nato, the North Atlantic Treaty Organization founded in 1949, who included the US.

*Mackenize King, as Canadian Prime Minister, effectively killed off the first Canadian free-trade agreement with the United States drafted in the spring of 1948.*

The continuing currency crisis was finally solved by the American launch of the Marshall Plan for European economic recovery. The same able Canadian negotiators convinced their American counterparts that Marshall Plan funds could be used by Europeans to purchase not only American but also Canadian goods—thus bringing US dollars into Canada. However, this did mark the beginning of the increasing domination of the Canadian economy by the American, as had been feared by King. The nationalists may not have liked the fact, but Canada's post-war boom was financed in part by the Marshall Plan and in part by US investment in Canada encouraged by the Canadian government at every opportunity. It was undoubtedly American investment that would allow Canadian manufacturing industry, and the Canadian mining, oil and gas industries, to expand and flourish in the 1950s and after. The outbreak of the Korean War in 1950 did much to quicken this, by increasing the US military and industrial demand for secure sources of the raw materials that Canada was well placed to provide.

* * *

Back in the Burns Brothers cage, the record keeping of this economic boom, in which share sales and purchases had to be precisely noted and balanced, was a tedious and complicated affair in the days before computers. My job was to post client share transactions and sales in the client ledger cards that were kept in the cage's vast filing cabinets. When someone bought shares, the date and the amount of the purchase were posted on the appropriate card, together with an identification of the share and the account number. When the selling broker or the stock exchange clearing house sent over the certificates, and when the client sent in the money, further entries were posted. The same process occurred with a sale. But the records seemed never to balance, and we would work late every night trying to do our job. I did not complain because I was paid some overtime, supper money and the fare home. (Sometimes, I was forced to walk a long way to work from Leaside, just to save the subway fare.)

Most of my record keeping concerned transactions of Bell Telephone corporate bonds and shares. After I had been at Burns for about five months, Bell Telephone had one of their many rights issues, where every shareholder was offered a 'right' to buy a certain extra number of Bell shares depending on the size of his or her shareholding. Some of the rights were registered in the shareholder's own name and others were not—they were registered either in the name of Burns Brothers or indeed to some other broker or owner. On top of this, some of the shareholders had bought Bell shares because they wanted the rights to buy more shares, others were selling their shares, and still others were selling only the rights because they did not want to buy more shares. The permutations made for unbelievably complicated record keeping and the system was in a mess. I was surrounded by paper, and I was in despair. Here I was in charge of the Bell Telephone rights cards, but there was not a chance, ever, of the figures balancing. I worked late, I did my best, but the task was impossible.

One lunchtime when I was having trouble balancing the records as usual, I had two batches of Bell rights cards placed near the window-sill. It was a hot summer's day in an office without air conditioning, so as I left for lunch I decided to let some air in. Our offices were on the 19th floor of the Bank of Nova Scotia building near King and Bay Street (the Canadian equivalent of Wall Street). As I raised the window, the suction pulled all of the cards outside and I could do absolutely nothing but watch helplessly as 40 or 50 large ledger cards floated away in the breeze. That was it, I thought, horrified—I'll be fired and my career will be over, ended before it had started by the very paper I had planned to use to my advantage. After lunch, I confessed what had happened to the cage manager and kept my head down for the rest of the afternoon, waiting and waiting to be hauled in. But nothing happened.

The next morning the office manager, not the cage manager, called me in to see him. He said he did not know what to do, so he suggested that I get all the Bell Telephone ledger cards and post the rights position from them. As for the missing cards, we knew what each shareholder had been offered by Bell, so I could post that figure. Buy and sell contracts would give us complete information on subsequent share and rights transactions. I worked day and night, and by 10.30 the following morning the Bell Telephone rights position balanced for the first time in the history of Burns! Nothing more was said, but a couple of weeks later I was moved out of the cage to the margin department—a promotion.

Six months later, I left Burns because I had realized it was the wrong place to be if I wanted to be a financier. I needed to learn more about Canada. So in 1957, I went to Montreal, and got a job selling advertising and writing a monthly arts column for the *Montrealer* magazine. This was a glamorous little consumer publication, covering all the arts, and it was fun to work for—but it could not pay me a salary, only a commission on the advertising I sold, and I was lucky if I made $50 a week. Even so, life was good and I worked hard there, until one day the advertising manager told me I was wasting my talents: I would do well if I went to Maclean Hunter, the biggest and best magazine publisher in Canada.

Following his tip, I wrote to the company asking for a job but was turned down flat because I lacked experience—a huge disappointment, since I had not even been interviewed. Undeterred, I borrowed a car, drove to Toronto and was lucky to get an appointment with a senior executive in charge of business publications. I told him about my financial background in London, and said that I wanted to make my career with Maclean Hunter and change my life. He heard me out and then told me to wait outside. In less than an hour, I was shown into the office of another man, a group manager, and told that I had a job.

*Style* magazine, where I now started work, was a Montreal-based trade magazine for the clothing and fashion industry. Less fun than working for a consumer magazine like the *Montrealer*, but with a real salary, $7,000 a year, which was very good pay in the late 1950s. My job was to sell advertising to the rag trade in Montreal, which was largely run by Jewish entrepreneurs. Theirs was a tough business—there is no glamour in glamour—and they were struggling to survive and frequently bad tempered. Sometimes they threw me out on a whim, but if I returned the following day, often they would see me and perhaps buy an advertisement. They forced me to be creative. I would usually prepare two advertisements so as to give them a choice. If they rejected one they would often buy the second. They taught me how to bargain as if I were in a bazaar. I soon found I could handle the rough and tumble and started to enjoy it. In fact I am certain that this early experience was tremendous training for my later career in the investment industry. Then another job came up at Maclean Hunter, with an industrial trade publication called *Plant Administration and Engineering*—a step up from *Style* in salary, if not in glamour. When I got this new job, my salary and commission increased to about $12,000 a year.

Life had already improved remarkably since my time in the Burns cage. Apart from the money, I was dressing well, meeting interesting people and skiing at St Saveur every weekend with my future wife Valda. We had met in 1958, got married soon afterwards and our first-born, David, arrived in 1960. But now I was actively searching for a major opportunity that would lead me back into the financial world.

Around this time, I read a newly published book, *Flame of Power: Intimate Profiles of Canada's Greatest Businessmen* by Peter C. Newman, a refugee from the Nazis who had escaped from Czechoslovakia as a child and come via Britain to Canada in the early 1940s, where he eventually made a name for himself as a business writer on *The Financial Post*, Canada's national investment and public affairs weekly. Newman's inside knowledge and lively (but never purple) style inspired me tremendously and made his book virtually my business bible. At just the right time in my life, it introduced me not only to eleven major personalities in Canadian business—five of whom were still alive at the time I read it—but also brought Canada's history and its recent past alive

*Peter C. Newman, a refugee from Czechoslovakia, came to Canada in the early 1940s and made a name for himself as a business writer on* The Financial Post.

for me. I had long been aware that to be a student of Canada was almost as vital to success as to be a student of finance. *Flame of Power* really got me going on my study of Canada, and provided many warnings and lessons, as well as much encouragement, during my early years there. Particularly satisfying to read was the book's conclusion that, "In survey after survey, men who have spent their professional lives analyzing national development trends have chosen Canada as the land with the most buoyant business future." Although I had decided to seek my fortune in Canada without the benefit of Newman's wonderful optimism (he also predicted that increased automation would usher in a 30-hour working week and a three-day weekend for many), his book confirmed that I was on the right track.

*Flame of Power* is so full of compelling insights and anecdotes that I cannot resist describing the book in some detail, picking out a few aspects that most influenced me.

The lead chapter, almost inevitably, is given over to the Canadian who most nearly approximated to the level of power held in the United States by Carnegie or Ford—Sir Herbert Holt. In 1926, the London-based *Daily Express* declared Holt to be a more important figure in Canada than the Prime Minister was in Britain.

Holt emigrated to Canada from Dublin in 1875, aged 19, and became a railway engineer in an age of heroic railway building. By 1883, he was in a position to form his own railway construction company and make a success of it. Then he moved to Montreal, became the largest shareholder in the Montreal Gas Company and merged it with the Royal Electric Company to form the tremendously successful company Montreal Light, Heat and Power Consolidated. From this base his empire expanded beyond railways and utilities until it included hotels, fur shops, flour mills and life insurance, among other kinds of business. By the 1920s, such was his one-man domination of goods and services that Montrealers grumbled: "We get up in the morning and switch on one of Holt's lights, cook breakfast on Holt's gas, smoke one of Holt's cigarettes, read the

*In 1926, the London-based* Daily Express *declared the tycoon Sir Herbert Holt to be a more important figure in Canada than the Prime Minister was in Britain.*

morning news printed on Holt's paper, ride to work on one of Holt's streetcars, sit in an office heated by Holt's coal, then at night go to a film in one of Holt's theatres."

It was not until 1902 that he moved into banking, taking on the presidency of the Royal Bank of Canada at a time when it had 100 branches and around $50 million in assets. By the end of his 26-year tenure, the bank had 688 branches and assets of $750 million. Holt's personal wealth grew commensurately, and by 1928 his fortune was estimated at three billion dollars—at a time when the Canadian government had only a tenth of this amount, $300 million, in circulation. Although his businesses were not invulnerable, for example his pulp and paper company was severely damaged by the depression of the 1930s, his personal fortune remained largely unaffected, as did his reputation as Canada's greatest money mogul.

As a man, Holt was a ruthless, solitary, publicity-phobic monomaniac with a face that "resembled nothing so much as a carefully washed and smoothly polished Irish potato punctured by pinched, garter-blue eyes"—

in Newman's memorable words. He concludes his chapter on Holt with this telling anecdote about Holt's death in 1941:

> Holt received his public elegy on the day of his death. During the International League baseball game at Montreal's Delorimier Stadium, the bottom of the fifth inning was interrupted by the rude blat of a loudspeaker announcing: "Sir Herbert Holt is dead."
>
> The crowd hushed, whispered. Then cheered.

Holt may have been the tycoon who had the greatest personal effect on the development of Canada as a nation, but he was far from being the only one with far-reaching ambitions. Another such was Donald Smith, later Lord Strathcona, a member of Parliament and the chief financier of the Canadian Pacific Railway (CPR). Born in Scotland in 1829, Smith spent his first three decades in Canada as a fur trader for the Hudson's Bay Company. It was during these wilderness years in Labrador that he "acquired the insensibility to both hatred and loyalty which later allowed him twice to betray his political allegiances and to promote some of the most questionable deals in Canadian business history," writes Newman. Smith's determination eventually saw him take control of the Hudson's Bay Company, and change its focus from fur to land. From there, with the help of the savings of many Hudson's Bay factors, who recognized and trusted his drive and talents, Smith managed to take charge of the Bank of Montreal and use it to dominate the financing of the CPR in the 1880s. His shares in this audacious construction project—the railway that opened up the Canadian West, and the first pan-Canadian corporation—rose from $25 at the beginning to $280 by the time of his death in 1914.

Knighted the year after the completion of the CPR in 1885, and raised to the peerage in 1897, the year of Queen Victoria's Diamond Jubilee, Lord Strathcona was regarded as an adventurous empire builder by his admirers and as a conniving self-seeker by his enemies. Without any

*Lord Strathcona driving in the last spike at Craigellachie, British Columbia, marking the completion of the Canadian Pacific Railroad joining the eastern seaboard with Vancouver on 7 November 1885.*

question, though, he was a great philanthropist, considerably more charitable than Holt, who believed that too much charity would stop people from working. Strathcona gave away twelve million dollars in the course of his life and another $20 million in his will. He is also remembered for establishing and equipping the celebrated cavalry unit known as Strathcona's Horse at the time of the Boer War.

If Lord Strathcona was the man who financed the CPR, then Sir William Van Horne was the man who built it. The classic photograph of the completion of the great railway on 7 November 1885 shows a bearded, top-hat-and-tailed Donald Smith (yet to be ennobled) uncomfortably bashing in the last spike with a hammer, watched at his right elbow by an unsmiling but obviously pleased Van Horne. Critics at the time dismissed the CPR as "absurd, a railroad built from the edge of civilization through wilderness to reach nowhere" (as summarized by Michael Bliss in *Northern Enterprise*), but Van Horne's management genius transformed it into a transport empire. When he died in 1915, writes Newman, "The entire CPR system was halted in silent homage for five minutes." (Cuba declared a day of national mourning. "He did more for us in one year," said the Republic's President, "than Spain did in four centuries.")

Van Horne had little formal education, having been expelled from school at fourteen, but he had formidable drive, which enabled him to defy geography, blasting his railway through the Rocky Mountains and steadying it along the soggy shore of Lake Superior. When the last of the 2,905 miles of track had been laid, Van Horne's development of the CPR into an integrated transport network opened up vast swathes of the continent. He encouraged teachers and doctors into the West by offering them free homes; he invested in wheat production, bidding half a dollar a bushel when brokers would pay only 35 cents; he set up Canada's first tourist trail, building a string of hotels at points along the track to encourage visitors; and he internationalized the CPR's business by

*When Sir William Cornelius Van Horne died in 1915, the entire Canadian Pacific Railroad system was halted in silent homage for five minutes.*

building a fleet of ocean liners. His boundless energy, his mastery of operational detail, his imagination and sheer optimism were extra-ordinary. Equally attractive were his discerning dedication to art, both as a collector and as an artist himself—a dozen of Van Horne's best paintings hang in the Montreal Museum of Fine Arts—and the sheer range of his interests: he was "the inventor of a grasshopper killer, an avalanche deflector, and a submarine finder, [who] even plotted the St Lawrence Seaway half a century before it was built," writes Newman. Of all the Canadian moguls, it is Van Horne with his restless curiosity and will to enjoy life who appeals most to me.

Among the more recent generation of businessmen profiled in *Flame of Power*, I was impressed by Sir James Dunn's patience and canniness. After much careful planning, Dunn took over the Algoma Steel Corporation when it was in receivership and turned it back into a proprietary, profitable steel firm. And also by the vision and ingenuity of the five Steinberg brothers of Montreal, who built their small family-run delicatessen into Canada's largest privately owned supermarket chain. But the contemporary figure who seemed closest to my own aspirations in the world of paper was Edward Plunket Taylor.

In the mid-1950s in Canada, E. P. Taylor was a household name whose figure, dressed in waistcoat and top hat, was instantly recognizable from gossip and sports magazines as well as the financial sections of the newspapers. But although he was familiar, frankly speaking his image was not a positive one. His name was frequently accompanied by unflattering epithets, such as "the beer baron", "E(xcess) P(rofits) Taylor" and even "the mad miser of millions". Taylor became a symbol of the potentially crushing power of big business, and it is certainly true that he believed in unbridled, unapologetic capitalism. In *Flame of Power*, Taylor is described as regarding "the free enterprise system primarily as a successful arrangement of human affairs in such a way that maximum benefits inevitably accrue to those who are the most adroit."

Taylor may not have been the most likeable of models, or someone to

*In the mid-1950's in Canada, E. P. Taylor became a symbol of the potentially crushing power of big business. He is pictured here in 1942 sitting on the left of Lord Beaverbrook (centre) at a meeting of the British Supply Council.*

be followed too faithfully, yet still there was much in the story of his rise and rise that I found inspiring and almost awe-inspiring. For a start, he did not inherit wealth, despite many myths to the contrary. Graduating from Ashbury College in 1922, his first ventures were a bus firm (where he and his business partner drove the converted trucks) and a taxi business, Red Line Taxi, which was sold for a profit and went on to become one of Ottawa's largest.

After this first success, however, Taylor went to work for his father's investment business, and at the same time his grandfather made him a director of his brewery. Beer would be the foundation of Taylor's empire. But the lubricant that enabled Taylor's empire to grow would not be beer, but paper. As *Flame of Power* explains, "Taylor assembled all available financial facts about the Ontario breweries, then calculated how individual circumstances could be used to obtain their control. Instead of cash, he planned to trade pieces of paper for the properties by issuing shares in his newly formed Brewing Corporation of Ontario." In 1930, with the backing of an American promoter, Clark Jennison, Taylor became the owner of seven small brewing plants and established the Brewing Corporation of Canada. In 1937, its name was changed to Canadian Breweries Limited.

From this relatively modest start, Taylor's astonishingly acquisitive and aggressive style expanded the business exponentially. He worked 16 hours a day, appropriating more and more plants. Within ten months, he had control of ten breweries and a soft-drinks firm; over the next 25 years, he grabbed 23 rival breweries, achieving an eleven-million-barrel brewing capacity, and increased his sales more than 20-fold, so that by 1952 his companies controlled half of Canadian beer sales. At the same time, he played a key civilian role in the Canadian war effort, coordinating industrial links between Canada, the United States and Britain. For this he was made a Companion of St Michael and St George in 1946—the highest royal order available to Canadian citizens.

But all this was not enough for Taylor. He could not quench his thirst for expansion. So he moved into malting and soy bean mills; he diversified into eastern forest industries (sawmills and hardwood distillation); and he developed what had been a peripheral interest in food and soft drinks into a nationwide web of bakeries, cafeterias, sweet shops and caterers through the companies Canadian Food Products Limited and Orange Crush.

Then, in 1945, on the model of the New York financier Floyd Odlum's Atlas Corporation, Taylor set up the Argus Corporation. The idea was to concentrate his assorted holdings in what was a modified version of a closed-end investment fund. Taylor himself described Argus as "a special-situations company set up to acquire a sufficiently large percentage of control in carefully selected operating companies to effect an important voice in policy decisions." Or in Newman's words: "In each of its extensions, Argus buys enough equity stock for effective control, but without tying up the excessive amounts of capital that would be needed to get absolute control." As the Canadian economy began to expand after the war, Argus did spectacularly well. *Northern Enterprise* spells it out: "In its first ten years, from 1945 to 1955, the Canadian economy grew by 10.8 per cent per annum in current [1987] dollars. Profits of Argus's three most important holdings, Canadian Breweries, Dominion Stores, and Massey-Ferguson grew by 15.5, 20.8 and 21.8 per cent per annum respectively."

I did not have the hubris, even in my early twenties, to try to model myself on E. P. Taylor's success. Nor did I ever wish to acquire his reputation as a ruthless business carnivore that was part of his legendary status. But I was fascinated by Argus's seemingly endless upward trajectory (with a few glaring failures to give hope to lesser businessmen). I longed to show the kind of creativity and adventurousness his career had showed, and his enviable business instinct—when asked how he knew which companies would grow Taylor replied: "It's a question of judgement. I remember in the old days the shares of streetcar companies were considered gilt-edge investments. Well, they dried out. Then there was a time when the railroads were blue chip. Now they're all having a tough time, except the CPR. I never went into either of those things. It's worked out pretty well for me." Finally, the fact that he founded his entire business on detailed knowledge, determination and, above all, shrewd issuing of paper, was enormously encouraging to me. Only on one point did I have serious reservations—Taylor's willingness to borrow money. Frightened off borrowing by my father's disastrous borrowing habit in Ceylon, I was determined that I would always try my best to avoid borrowing.

*Flame of Power* fuelled my determination to get into the financial world. I made new contacts at Maclean Hunter and got to know the advertising manager at *The Financial Post* in Toronto, where Peter C. Newman had formerly been the assistant editor. I made an approach to him for a job, which he initially rejected as there was nothing available. But eventually *The Financial Post* did contact me and offered me a job selling advertising in Toronto, at a salary barely one half my very comfortable remuneration with *Plant Administration and Engineering* in Montreal. But a job on *The Financial Post* was a job in the centre of the financial industry in Toronto, where I wanted to be, and after talking things over with my wife, we decided that I should make the break. So in 1962, our family, with a new young daughter, Sarah, moved back to Toronto and I now had a new stature, working for a well-recognized business publication. The difference was immediately obvious. Before, when making a sales appointment, I would phone and say "This is Christopher Ondaatje of Plant Administration and Engineering" and they would say "Who?", but when I said "This is Christopher Ondaatje from The Financial Post", the response was "Oh, yes." Although I was not yet exactly where I wanted to be, I was at least in the right industry.

After a while, the paper sponsored me to take a course on Canadian securities for about six months. This particular course was a compulsory for anyone working in the investment industry in sales, research or merchant banking and had also become very popular with outsiders wanting a solid grounding in the workings of the stock market: the different types of financial instrument available and how each type of instrument worked in the market. This information was what truly interested me, and I got a real kick out of the course, as I had ten years earlier from the Institute of Bankers examination and the lecture at the London School of Economics. Studying for the Canadian securities course was fascinating, not 'work' at all, and I virtually memorized the information. When I took the exam in 1964, I got very high marks. My appetite for applying my knowledge of paper and money to real business became even stronger.

I now understood in considerable detail the makeup of the Canadian capital markets (both government and corporate), the fixed-income and equity stock markets, the various types of financial institutions and their role in the economy. And I was familiar with the different types of bonds with their varying terms to maturity, such as collateral bonds, some of which are protected by claims on specific assets of a corporation while others have a claim on all its assets, and with the different grades of bonds that depend on the financial health of a corporation. As for shares, it was the Canadian securities course that first opened my eyes to the true importance of preference shares. I already knew that preference shares—with their preferential treatment in the event of insolvency and their fixed rate of dividend—were less risky than ordinary shares, as mentioned in chapter two; now I began fully to appreciate their other advantage. Preference shares can be converted into riskier ordinary shares, with the potential for variable, potentially higher dividends, at a predetermined price and for a stated period of time. The skill lies in getting or demanding the valuable convertibility feature at an attractive price when arranging a corporate financing. We shall revisit preference shares in the story of the Pagurian Corporation in chapter five.

Through my job at *The Financial Post* in the first half of the 1960s, I continued to try to learn as much about Canada, its resources, and its potential for investment, as I knew about finance. New discoveries of raw materials and new ways to exploit old discoveries were the most seminal Canadian economic development of the 1950s and 1960s. The other major development was the construction of the St Lawrence Seaway with millions of dollars of Canadian and American money, completed in 1959, which acted as a spur to the natural resource development.

Before the Second World War, there was scarcely any iron-ore production in Canada. Then, in the post-war period, the exploitation of iron-ore deposits at Steep Rock Lake, west of Superior, and later of huge deposits of low-grade iron ore in the remote Quebec-Labrador region, turned Canada into one of the largest iron-ore producers in the world. The impetus came from the United States, where the Mesabi ores had become exhausted. The catch was how to move the Canadian iron ore to market. The St Lawrence Seaway—connecting the Atlantic Ocean with the Great Lakes via the St Lawrence River—solved the problem by enabling ocean-going ore carriers from Labrador to travel down the St Lawrence to the giant integrated steel mills located on the Great Lakes in both Canada and the US.

Other new mineral exploitation in this period involved nickel, a key constituent of stainless steel and of new industrial applications needed by the military, mined by companies such as Inco; and uranium, which made the fortunes of Stephen Roman at Consolidated Denison Mines. Canada, after the war, was the largest world supplier of nickel, and its sales of uranium to the United States government became one of its highest-earning export commodities. Finally there were the discoveries of vast new oil and gas fields in western Canada—in Alberta, with Calgary as the financial centre—which gave an immense boost to the economies of that region. At the end of the war, Canada produced only 23,000 barrels of oil a day. By 1953, with the increased production from Alberta, the total was over 222,000 barrels.

Iron, nickel, uranium, oil and gas overshadowed the more traditional natural resources, but these continued to be important. Pulp and paper accounted for about a quarter of Canadian export earnings in the mid-1950s. Hydroelectric power production grew, too, partly to feed the energy-intensive demands of aluminium production, in which Canada was now second only to the USA. The aluminium industry opened up new geographical areas close to cheap sources of hydroelectric power in Quebec and British Columbia, where there was little competition for the electricity.

As well as heavy industry, I needed to be aware, too, of the consumer, of social trends and lifestyle changes. The oil and gas discoveries caused Canadian homes to change from coal to oil and gas as their principal fuel in the 1950s, for example. But the biggest change was the move to suburban living. The need for suburban housing and new shopping centres made fortunes for real-estate developers and retailers. The migration from the city centres to the suburbs left housing in the city centres to be filled by the influx of new immigrants from Europe such as myself. They mingled and helped to break down earlier, old-boy and Wasp (White Anglo-Saxon Protestant) networks. In real estate, Jews and Eastern Europeans were now the dominant players. The 42-storey cruciform tower opened at Place Ville-Marie in Montreal in 1962, which instantly became a city landmark, exemplified the social changes of the time. Michael Bliss in *Northern Enterprise* describes its construction thus: "The building on Place Ville-Marie was a fair symbol of breakthrough. It was a collaboration between an American Jew, William Zeckendorf, his Chinese-American architect, I. M. Pei, and Scots-blooded Canadians, Donald Gordon of the CNR and James Muir of the Royal Bank, to erect a building with a French name."

Working at *The Financial Post*, I could naturally keep a sharp eye on the activities of the captains of commerce—the McConnells of Montreal in mining, the Irvings in oil refining, and of course Lord Beaverbrook, who, though he was living in England, still had substantial interests in Canada. I also observed the bankers. In the 1950s, the five chartered banks were the most powerful but also the most conservative of all the corporations. As Bliss remarks, "The traditional branch manager of a chartered bank developed a mentality not unlike the community librarian: the books and the money were to be kept as safely away from the public as possible." This attitude changed in the 1960s as the banks realized that other institutions, the consumer finance companies, were trying to eat their lunch by offering finance to the ordinary Canadian consumer—a type of client the major banks had hitherto shied away from. In the 1960s, the banks tackled the consumer loan business and put the consumer finance companies virtually out of business. The Canadian banks—as demonstrated by the success of bankers like Sir Herbert Holt and Lord Strathcona—have somehow always had an uncanny ability to remain profitable and growing, regardless of the economic environment or the competition.

Canadian politics was less immediately relevant to my interests, though I kept myself informed and in 1961 I became a Canadian citizen (while still retaining my British passport). The late 1950s and 1960s were an unstable period in Canada, politically speaking. The instability began in 1956, the year of my arrival, with an economic issue: how to finance the Trans-Canada Pipeline that would make available the new oil wealth of the West. The Conservative opposition charged that the Liberal government was giving the project away to the Americans. The government was mauled in Parliament over the issue and defeated in the 1957 election by the prairie populist John Diefenbaker, who now formed a minority government and remained as Prime Minister until 1963. However in the decade after the 1957 election, there were five federal elections, two changes of government and four minority governments. Yet this uncertain political climate seemed to have no effect on the economy. The 1960s, up to the centennial of the Canadian Confederation in 1967 with its famous Expo in Montreal, and the arrival of Pierre Trudeau on the political landscape, saw the longest sustained boom in the country's history, with low inflation and high growth that surpassed the expansion of the immediate post-war period.

The next step in my own career came in the middle of this boom. In 1964, just after my second daughter Jans was born and while selling advertising for *The Financial Post*, I bumped into Charles Loewen, a senior partner with Pitfield, Mackay, Ross and Company, one of the top investment houses of the day. I had first met him when I was starting out at the *Montrealer*. 'Chuck' Loewen was now considered to be one of the brightest and best in the industry. We became friendly and talked about my ambition to get into the investment business. But the job he got for me in retail sales would have required the completion of time-consuming courses and a substantial cut in salary. It was not where I wanted to be, so I did not take up his initial offer. We stayed in touch, though, and by the following year Chuck had organized one of the first institutional sales and research teams in Canada, which had already developed a loyal following in the institutional investment community. Chuck then offered me a job in institutional sales, again with a substantial cut in salary from *The Financial Post*—and this time I jumped at the opportunity. I could see that the new setup at Pitfield Mackay Ross might be the break into the world of paper and money I had been waiting for. It was a department organised to deal exclusively with sophisticated money managers—the most powerful on Bay Street.

When I told *The Financial Post* I was leaving, they seemed genuinely concerned that I was throwing away a chance to become a future vice-president of Maclean Hunter. I knew this was quite likely if I stayed around, but it was not the career I wanted. My newspaper job had given me an in-depth knowledge of Canada, its people and its financial structure, which was invaluable. But since I wanted to be on the inside of the financial world, not on the outside looking in, it was time to move on. I was willing to take the big cut in salary because I was not fascinated with money for its own sake, but much more with the power of paper.

My new life in the financial industry started in early 1966. I was one of the first to be hired by Chuck Loewen for the new institutional sales division. It was enormously successful and within three years we were the most profitable part of the company, employing twelve members of staff. I was at long last doing what I had wanted—dealing in paper to make money. Just thinking about the stock exchange was so stimulating that I could hardly wait to get up each morning. I was selling stocks to powerful men who controlled millions of dollars. Our clients valued our detailed research and advice, because it was formulated specifically for them, not for the broad interests of the firm's retail clients, which would have diluted its value. My salary cut turned out to be irrelevant, since at the end of the year I received a bonus that was a multiple of my salary. In 1966, I earned more money than I had believed possible when I arrived in the country just ten years before, somewhere around $35,000. But this was only the beginning. I knew that very soon I could begin to realize my real dream—to start my own business.

CHAPTER 5

# The Pagurian Story: An Empire of Paper

*Members of a species of hermit crab . . . exchange homes so that both end up with a better deal. Brian Hazlett from the University of Michigan watched the crabs, of the species* Pagurus marshi, *in his marine laboratory. A crab looking for a new home approached another crab bearing an ideal residence on its back and began knocking on the shell. Often an exchange took place, but sometimes it did not.*

Report in *The Globe and Mail*, Toronto, 1984

The company I founded, Pagurian—a name with an intentionally exotic, un-Canadian ring that I coined myself from the intriguing shell-trading habits of the *Pagurus* hermit crab—began life as an insignificant book publishing company, Pagurian Press. Like many a previous entrepreneur, going right back to Gutenberg and his printing press in Mainz in the 1450s, I was drawn to book publishing for its unique mixture of commerce, influence, aesthetics, risk and glamour. From 1967, over several years, I ran Pagurian Press virtually single-handed from my house in Toronto with my wife as editor and some freelance help, backed by a small group of private shareholders. In those early years I did not take any remuneration from the company, and its helter-skelter existence provided a few of us with much fun, many games and not too much risk.

As the company began to expand in the early 1970s, I added my interest in art to its activities, having realized that newly affluent Canadians would want historical and contemporary prints by Canadian artists on the walls of their new suburban homes. Pagurian Press moved into the publishing of Canadian art books and signed prints, and the collecting and selling of maps of Canada; and in the early 1980s Pagurian acquired its own art gallery in a fashionable part of Toronto, which we also used for talks, launch parties and the annual company meeting. (The art collection it accumulated, besides elegantly decorating the company's annual reports, was eventually worth more than $10 million.) The increasing cash flow from publishing books and art enabled me to buy minority shareholdings in other carefully selected companies, which continued to prosper under their own management while at the same time increasing the assets of Pagurian. This unusual business model— the romance of using small-scale publishing to create wealth on a grander scale—fascinated a few people enough to invest in Pagurian's shares. They must also have noticed that I was steadily and patiently developing a sure instinct for the stock market, guided to some extent by my fast-growing investment experience as a partner of Loewen, Ondaatje, McCutcheon and Company, a surprisingly successful investment brokerage company founded with Charles Loewen and Fred McCutcheon when the three of us left Pitfield, Mackay, Ross and Company in late 1969.

A decade later, when Pagurian went public and was listed on the Toronto Stock Exchange in 1979, it was already beginning to delve into corporate finance. After that, so rapidly did the company outgrow its original publishing 'shell', that it dropped its only modestly profitable book publishing (while continuing to publish fine-art reproductions)— and dealt only in corporate finance. By the mid-1980s, in a period of worldwide boom in the stock markets, the Pagurian Corporation, following a series of high-value investments in other companies, had transformed itself into a small empire of paper investments with well over a thousand public shareholders—though its staff numbers were still tiny—and interests in the United States and Europe, as well as Canada. When I decided to sell the company at the end of 1988, Pagurian's after-tax earnings were more than $89 million, and the company had assets of over $550 million. (*NB* All dollars mentioned in this chapter are Canadian dollars.) I am still amazed to think that all this had grown from practically nothing: less than $2000 of profit from a single book, published in 1967. But such is the power of paper.

\*   \*   \*

The year 1967 was an important one for Canada: it was the centenary of the Confederation of 1867, the date when the country formally came into existence. Plans to celebrate the event had been announced by the government well in advance, and everyone was aware of it. Some time in 1963, I was on a business trip when I remember phoning my wife in Toronto and telling her I had a great idea for a book. In my continuing quest to learn about Canada, I used to spend hours in bookshops and libraries. Browsing through their stock, I realized that a vital piece of Canadian history had not been gathered into one volume for the general public. No easily readable book profiling all of the Prime Ministers of Canada—from Sir John A. Macdonald (1867–73/1878–91) to Lester B. Pearson (1963–68)—was available. There was an opportunity here, not only to fulfil a public need and make a little money for myself, but also, perhaps, to make a bit of a name as a New Canadian.

With some conscientious researchers, I spent the next three years assembling a simple book of profiles entitled *The Prime Ministers of Canada, 1867–1967*, timed to coincide with Canada's centennial celebrations. Then I approached established publishers with the manuscript but was either rebuffed or offered insulting advances; McLelland and Stewart, and also Macmillan, offered a $500 advance against a 10 per cent royalty on the first 5,000 copies sold—the usual sort of terms for a first-time author. After working hard to get the book together, I was not going to give it away for $500. So I decided—to hell with established publishers: I would become a publisher myself after raising from friends and colleagues the $3000 needed to pay the printing costs. We would share in the profits only after the $3000 had been repaid.

I put the $3000 in the bank and arranged for a commercial printer to print 3,000 copies of the book under the imprint Canyon Press—a reference to the 'canyons' between the high-rise financial buildings in Toronto's Bay Street area. As I did not have to pay the printer for 90 days and had an agreement with the book's distributor that he would pay me for the entire print run in 60 days, I immediately had a positive cash flow, which earned some interest for me. As I was to learn, positive cash flow is one of the vital components of financial success, and it has always struck me as an exciting concept. In this case, it meant that not only could I make money by publishing books, I could also make money with money sitting in the bank, held in trust until I had to pay my suppliers. So long as I hawkishly watched the cash flow and did not borrow, I had total freedom to run my little business without interference from creditors. From the very beginning, not borrowing was very important to me, and I am certain that it was a founding principle in Pagurian's eventual success.

To help sales, I circulated a letter to a host of people announcing the forthcoming publication of *The Prime Ministers of Canada, 1867–1967* and asking if they would like to buy a copy, priced $5.95. One letter somehow found its way to the desk of Stephen Roman, the uranium baron. The phone rang and I was told that Roman wanted to buy 1000 copies of the book. Thrilled, I offered him a discount price of $3 per copy and this was accepted. So in one phone call I had recouped the initial $3000 outlay. The copies that Roman bought went to all the members of the Canadian Parliament and Senate, together with a letter from him pasted into the prelims. Our remaining 2,000 copies sold out immediately and we rushed to do another printing. At the same time, I paid the printers their $3000 and in mid-1967 announced my intention to form a publishing company, Pagurian Press. I held 90 per cent of the shares of the company, and the other ten per cent was sold to shareholders in exchange for preference shares, raising $10,000 for Pagurian. In the new company's first annual report, covering 1967, as Pagurian's new president I wrote cautiously:

> The Company also during this period acquired a 52 per cent interest in *The Prime Ministers of Canada, 1867–1967* which by the year end had realized a return of $1481.00 on its investment. Taking a conservative view, the Company has written off an equal amount against its investment so that the book to date has yielded no net return. However the outlook for the publication over the long term is very good and it was on this basis that the investment was made.

In due course, *The Prime Ministers of Canada* became a school textbook, and by the time it stopped being reprinted and updated in the mid-1980s, it had sold over 600,000 copies. I remember that there was another centennial book, entitled *Mr Prime Minister*, which came out from another publisher. Written by a well-known political journalist, Bruce Hutchison, it was a superb book, far more sophisticated than Pagurian's book; but I doubt whether it sold as many as our small volume in its first year.

That same year, I ran into a new book published in New York that was of immense help to me in deciding what Pagurian should publish if it were to survive and prosper commercially. *70 Years of Best Sellers 1895–1965* by Alice Payne Hackett does what the title says: it gives the titles of the best-selling books in both fiction and (from 1917 onwards) non-fiction for each year in this 70-year period and, where available and reliable, actual sales figures.

Hackett's book also comments on the titles for each year and provides analyses of best-selling books by genre: religious books, cookbooks, crime and suspense books, children's books, reference books and others. Under "Cookbooks", she notes: "Next to the Bible and books on religious subjects, cookbooks have been the most consistent sellers in non-fiction since 1895. It is apparent from a study of the best-seller lists

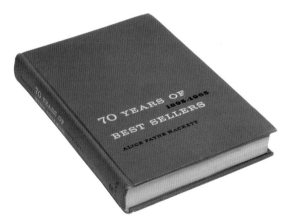

*70 Years of Best Sellers 1895–1965 by Alice Payne Hackett was of immense help to me in deciding what Pagurian Press should publish if it were to survive and prosper commercially.*

that only the need for advice on feeding the spirit surpasses the need for advice—and books—on feeding the body." And in the book's introduction, she concludes by quoting a perceptive statement from the American academic James Hart, taken from his study *The Popular Book: A History of America's Literary Taste* (published by Oxford University Press in 1950):

> The book that time judges to be great is occasionally also the book popular in its own period; but, by and large, the longer-lived work reflects the demands of the moment only in the most general sense. Usually the book that is popular pleases the reader because it is shaped by the same forces that mould his non-reading hours, so that its dispositions and convictions, its language and subject, recreate the sense of the present, to die away as soon as that present becomes the past. Books of that sort generally are unreadable for succeeding ages; but like other fragments of the past, they help form the present. The volumes themselves may gather dust on library shelves, but they have left lasting impression on the American mind, etched deeply into a national consciousness.

I would not claim "greatness" for a single one of the 612 books published by Pagurian Press (as many as 60 titles in one year) during the decade or so from 1967, in the sense of a classic Hemingway novel or a book like E. H. Gombrich's *The Story of Art*. The vast majority were forgettable—indeed I suspect that if someone wrote a history of publishing in Canada, Pagurian might even be omitted altogether. In the first place, we avoided fiction. This was partly because to publish commercial fiction would have risked treading on the toes of the highly successful romance publisher Harlequin Books, whose owners I knew well (in the 1970s, Loewen Ondaatje McCutcheon helped Harlequin financially, as we shall soon see), and partly because I knew I was not sophisticated enough to choose fiction writers who would be a success. Instead, Pagurian published non-fiction. Like the stock market, non-fiction has a historical record showing the kinds of books that always sell, and I depended on it, while at the same time aiming to give many of our books a specifically Canadian flavour.

Looking back, I do think Pagurian published a few books of lasting merit, however. Notably two highly illustrated books on the history and old houses of Toronto, and two art books by one of Canada's best-known and best-loved artists, William Kurelek, whom I got to know personally in his studio in Toronto: *Kurelek's Canada* and *The Last of the Arctic*, both of which were my idea. Besides being attractive and original books, Kurelek's books helped to sell large numbers of prints of the paintings in the books, which Kurelek personally signed. Although the Canadian art world criticized Pagurian for selling prints that were not 'real', the artist himself was content with our business arrangement, in fact he specifically encouraged me to sell his signed prints as widely as possible throughout Canada. Kurelek died of cancer in 1977, not long after the Arctic book appeared, when he was only 50 years old. I have a feeling that he already knew he was dying when we collaborated on his second book.

And even if very few Pagurian books were destined to endure, we definitely did publish dozens of books that successfully reflected James

*Besides being attractive and original books,* Kurelek's Canada *and* The Last of the Arctic *helped to sell large numbers of prints of the paintings in the books, which Kurelek personally signed.*

Hart's "demands of the moment" and a handful that might even be said to have had some small influence on Canada's "national consciousness". *The Prime Ministers of Canada* would be one of this handful, as would be *The Black Donnellys: The True Story of Canada's Most Barbaric Feud* by Thomas P. Kelley, and so too would be a couple of Pagurian's cookbooks: *The Edible Wild* by Berndt Berglund and Clare E. Bolsby and the *Encyclopedia of Canadian Cooking* by Jehane Benoit.

*The Edible Wild* was a wilderness survival book. An old Swede, Berndt Berglund, came to see me one day and said he wanted to do a book. "What do you know about?" I asked him. "I am a woodsman. I know all about logging." "But that's not going to sell . . . What do you eat?" "We eat everything—anything we can get. We eat porcupines—leaves, roots, anything the birds eat. We eat the wilderness." "Can you do a cookbook?" "I can't do a cookbook, but I've got a girlfriend who knows how to cook and I can do the book with her." So Berglund and his girlfriend Clare Bolsby put the book together, I chose the title, and the book sold like hotcakes in Canada and became the first title I sold to Scribners, the famous New York publishers. When it appeared in the US, the Scribners sales manager introduced me to Charles Scribner himself who asked me: "What if anybody dies from one of these recipes?" I had no answer. There was a pause, then Scribner said: "Well I guess if they do, we won't hear from them anyway, will we?"

Madame Jehane Benoit was a cook famous in French Canada but not known at all in English Canada, who looked as if she enjoyed her food. I invited her from Montreal to Toronto for a chat. When she arrived, we sat together on the single bed in her Four Seasons motel room and we got on very well. I seduced her into turning her loose-leaf recipes written in French into a book in English on Canadian cooking. Our initial print run of the *Encyclopedia of Canadian Cooking* was 15,000 copies, but the book kept selling, heading for the 100,000 mark. Madame Benoit published two or three more cookbooks with Pagurian after the encyclopedia.

*Madame Jehane Benoit was a cook famous in French Canada but not known at all in English Canada until Pagurian published her* Encyclopedia of Canadian Cooking.

Much less successful commercially, but important to me personally, was one of our many sports books, published in 1967. Most of these were about hockey, had plenty of illustrations and were written by a familiar sports personality. *Olympic Victory* was my own book, written with Gordon Currie. He and I had been members of the Canadian bob-sled team at the Winter Olympics held in Innsbruck in 1964. This determined adventure was crowned by our Canadian team winning an Olympic gold medal, although sadly I have to admit that I was not personally part of the winning sled. *Olympic Victory* sold modestly but received warm reviews from some severe critics.

I also ventured into fiction in 1974, but my semi-autobiographical novel, *Fool's Gold: The First Million*, quoted in chapter two, was published under a (totally transparent) pseudonym, Simon Marawille, and the publisher was Scribners, not Pagurian Press. I thought I could write a novel—but I discovered I could not. The book is a crude effort in terms of its characterization, but I still think the plot is fairly exciting. And the fact is that the novel sold well; Scribners were disappointed when I asked them not to reprint it. Crude though it is, I feel that *Fool's Gold*

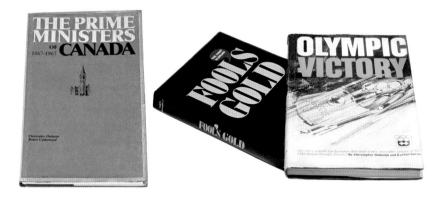

The Prime Ministers of Canada, 1867–1967, Fool's Gold *and* Olympic Victory *were my first books published in Canada and the United States. Eventually,* The Prime Ministers of Canada *sold over 600,000 copies.*

does catch the atmosphere of Toronto's Bay Street in the late 1960s, especially the panic during the stock-market correction of 1969 that lost many of my friends a lot of money and was a salutary warning for me at a time when my partners and I were planning to leave Pitfield Mackay Ross and set up Loewen Ondaatje McCutcheon. Although the rapid financial rise and fall of the novel's central character did not reflect what happened to me, it might have done—had I chosen to gamble on the Canadian stock market rather than patiently and cautiously building up Pagurian as I actually did. In a sense, the plot and emotions of the novel were a way of helping me to deal with my biggest fears as a financier.

Much of the stock-market information in the book is accurate, including the key facts on which the most dramatic episode turns. This involves trading in a then fairly recent European invention, Velcro, that had been licensed to a Canadian company Velok Limited in 1957. In the late 1960s, Velcro took off as a product after the US government's decision to use it in the Apollo space programme, and this made the Canadian licensee's shares a hot property in the stock market. The novel's central character Michael de Shane and two stockbroker friends get wind of the crucial decision in advance and decide to pool all the funds they have or can borrow, buy Velcro shares, and then hang on to them as the price rockets after the government's public announcement. I myself had Velcro shares at this time and my stake went up and then down, but unlike de Shane, who tries to commit suicide when he loses his recently acquired first million in the stock-market correction, I did not get into deep trouble. Perhaps I was lucky that I did not have much spare cash at the time to invest in Velcro, but I doubt I would have fallen for a huge speculation like my central character. By nature, I much prefer to take a calculated risk, rather than a high-rolling gamble.

A truer insight into my career as a financier than *Fool's Gold* might be J. Paul Getty's book *How To Be Rich*, based on a series of his articles commissioned by *Playboy* magazine. The book appeared in 1966 and

*J. Paul Getty's* How To Be Rich, *published in 1966, taught me the importance of research. He may not have been a particularly attractive individual—but he was a brilliant investor.*

I read it assiduously, as I had *Flame of Power*, *The Age of the Moguls* and *The Robber Barons*. Getty may not have been a particularly attractive individual—few of the men in those three books are—but he was a brilliant investor. His father was a self-made man in the oil business and his son's experience began in the oil fields of Oklahoma as a wildcatter in 1914. However Getty worked largely independently of his father and of established businesses, made himself a millionaire and retired at the age of 24. But then his restlessness, together with his belief that success should not be driven entirely by the desire to amass a fortune (hence his decision *not* to call his book *How To Get Rich*), pushed him back into the oil industry, where he became a billionaire and the world's richest man.

Getty's book taught me the importance of research—he was his own geologist, legal adviser and explosives expert, whose preferred reading was oil industry reports. He also espoused many sensible business principles, whatever the nature of the business (including the advice to

166

invest in a business you know and understand). Getty's ten points to consider when evaluating a stock purchase were, and are, a first-rate formula for sound investment, which I followed and which undoubtedly contributed to Pagurian's success. These are the questions Getty advises the investor to ask about a company he is planning to invest in:

1. What is the company's history? Is it a solid and reputable firm, and does it have able, efficient and seasoned management?

2. Is the company producing or dealing in goods or services for which there will be a continuing demand in the foreseeable future?

3. Is the company in a field that is not dangerously overcrowded, and is it in a good competitive position?

4. Are company policies and operations farsighted and aggressive without calling for unjustified and dangerous over-expansion?

5. Will the corporate balance sheet stand up under the close scrutiny of a critical and impartial auditor?

6. Does the corporation have a satisfactory earnings record?

7. Have reasonable dividends been paid regularly to stockholders? If dividend payments were missed, were there good and sufficient reasons?

8. Is the company well within safe limits in so far as both long- and short-term borrowing are concerned?

9. Has the price of the stock moved up and down over the past few years without violently wide and apparently inexplicable fluctuations?

10. Does the per-share value of the company's net realizable assets exceed the stock exchange value of a common-stock [i.e. ordinary] share at the time the investor contemplates buying?

It is very easy to get bogged down in the intricacies of the financial world and forget these basic principles. Without them, I would not have succeeded in investing in paper as I did. However, I do have my own top

ten tips based on my accumulated experience. Some are original, some adapted from other sources, and all are epigrammatic, as a deliberate contrast to Getty's sober wisdom:

1. Investors bank on the climate. Speculators gamble on the weather.
2. You never go broke taking profits.
3. If you don't know what to do—do nothing.
4. Never let the sun go down on a good bid.
5. If it looks too good to be true—it usually is.
6. Just because you make a few good investment decisions doesn't mean you are a genius.
7. All I want is an unfair advantage.
8. If you want to be successful you've got to have friends. If you want to be very successful you've got to have enemies.
9. History repeats itself—especially in the financial world.
10. You will never beat the market.

Many of these thoughts first occurred to me while I was working at Loewen Ondaatje McCutcheon, as I applied principles such as Getty's in the stock market of the 1970s and 1980s. LOM opened its doors for business in January 1970. The original idea of forming our own institutional boutique came from Charles Loewen, who had first employed me at Pitfield Mackay Ross. The third member of the trio, Fred McCutcheon, working at Pitfield Mackay Ross too, was the son of Wallace McCutcheon of Argus Corporation (E. P. Taylor's company) who was also a former Diefenbaker cabinet minister. The three of us were equal partners, investing $135,000 each for a 25 per cent share of the firm; the other key members of LOM held the remaining 25 per cent. A number of sales personnel and research analysts at Pitfield Mackay Ross followed us to LOM. In addition, we hired the best analysts, the best traders and some of the best sales people on Bay Street.

*Ed Franklin of the Toronto* Globe and Mail *drew this cartoon in 1981 of Loewen Ondaatje McCutcheon & Company Limited, founded in January 1970.*

The formation and expansion of LOM took place at the worst possible time in the North American economy. The Vietnam War was revving up in the late 1960s and the guns-before-butter economic policies of the Johnson Administration in the United States had driven up American inflation and stalled the economy. Then the US Federal Reserve raised interest rates and killed the stock market. Regardless, Bay Street wanted to do business with us. Almost immediately in 1970, LOM was an enormous success. We three were already well known from our days together at Pitfield Mackay Ross. Now, as a small, new, independent brokerage boutique, we had none of the conflicts experienced in the large integrated houses. Ours was a fresh approach, in which we provided sophisticated, independent research for institutions and were not beholden to merchant-banking clients or to the retail stock trade that is normally a key area for the integrated houses. We could call the shots on stock recommendations as we saw them and be totally objective—and our advice made money. Clients came to trust our judgement, and so they made sure that we were well looked after. For several years, LOM was the most influential of the institutional brokers in Canada, as demonstrated by the way in which other firms sprang up in the 1970s using our model, which also professed to be institutional boutiques. My share in LOM turned out to be a very good investment—eventually worth many millions of dollars to me when I sold my stake in the company to the new LOM president in 1988.

One of our first major deals for LOM involved book publishing. In 1970, Harlequin Books, the leading Canadian romance publisher, wanted to buy Mills and Boon, its supplier and perhaps the world's most famous publisher of romantic fiction. With my limited but first-hand experience with Pagurian, admittedly not in romantic fiction, I could see that Harlequin had a winning formula—pulp romantic fiction for an insatiable market, almost entirely women—and with this conviction I was able to help raise four million dollars from others for Harlequin to make the purchase. Then a few years after this successful acquisition, in 1975,

LOM negotiated the sale of a controlling interest in Harlequin to *The Toronto Star*. Canada's biggest-selling newspaper wanted to buy not just a majority stake in Harlequin or a passive investment but all of the shares outstanding in the company. This required LOM to put together small shareholdings in the book publisher, which could be sold to *The Toronto Star*. In the course of doing all these small deals, I marvelled at—and inwardly digested—the fact of how very much more money can be made when you control a deal than when you are just a part of one. Enormous profits are made when shares are worth much more to one company or individual for ownership purposes (in this case, *The Toronto Star*) than they are in the general market place. The eventual total purchase of Harlequin was expensive for *The Toronto Star*—and lucrative for LOM— but it turned out to be one of the newspaper's shrewder moves, since Harlequin is today a cash cow, making more than $75 million in profits annually, and is a major factor in the paper's survival.

In the beginning, LOM used other dealers to trade on the floor of the Toronto Stock Exchange and do the clearing. But as we matured, we developed our own trading and floor-trading group and our own back office (with a 'cage' of the kind where I had once worked). We opened an office in Montreal and then in Vancouver. One day, out of the blue, we received a phone call from Christian Pinchart-Deny, manager of the Paris office of Dominion Securities, telling us that he and three of his partners had decided to leave Dominion and wanted to become part of our group. Dominion was at this time by far the most important French-based Canadian broker dealing in Canadian securities. I suppose these very talented Frenchmen were attracted to LOM because of our independence, our reputation and, not least, by the prospect of keeping a larger proportion of the profits made by their efforts for themselves.

So in early 1974, LOM went international. We gave our French office complete autonomy in running its own affairs with the backing of what was considered to be the best sales, research and trading group in Canada. The day after Pinchart-Deny and his partners agreed to leave Dominion and join us, now having no place to hang their hats they telephoned us from phone booths in Paris with orders from loyal clients eager to support their new enterprise. For much of the 1970s and 1980s, our French office must have transacted over 90 per cent of the buying and selling of Canadian equities by French institutions.

LOM put up all the money to get the Paris office started and agreed to distribute 25 per cent of the profits generated there to the Paris staff—a significant income from the very beginning. Shortly after the Paris office was opened, LOM opened in Geneva too, which further helped to increase its presence in Europe. But the new European offices had an even greater value to me personally, above and beyond my personal stake in LOM. My French colleagues would in due course play an important role in introducing Pagurian's shares to European investors. Without LOM's French operation, the international expansion of Pagurian would not have been possible, and I would never have had the unique thrill of dealing in paper not just in Canada but also in the international financial scene.

By the end of 1978, Pagurian's paper investments were worth nearly $5.3 million, which generated an investment income that year of almost $1.3 million. This was ten times our income from publishing. I therefore judged that the time had come to get out of book publishing—which was anyway suffering severely from the high North American interest rates and high paper prices—and focus more on corporate investment and corporate finance. Publishing had provided Pagurian with cash flow, and by controlling our cash flow ruthlessly, and—most importantly—never borrowing, the company had grown steadily over twelve years. At any time of the day (and even during sleepless nights), I knew almost to the nearest dollar how much the company was worth and what fractions of it were in cash, shares and other assets. I also knew that if I continued to apply the business discipline and acumen that had worked for us during the 1970s, Pagurian would continue to expand and could become profitable on a much large scale.

It was at this point, during 1979–80—the pivotal years in the Pagurian story for several reasons—that it became a public company listed on the Toronto Stock Exchange. In taking this necessary and important step in 1979, I restructured the company so that there were two classes of ordinary shares: class A, which did not have a vote, and class B, which did have a vote. I personally owned 83 per cent all of the class B (voting) shares and 53 per cent of the class A (non-voting) shares at the time we went public. This structure was essential to me. It ensured that in the years to come, as Pagurian issued more class A shares to finance its ambitious investment plans, I would not lose control of the company. Control of voting in Pagurian was as important in my long-term plans as avoidance of debt in financing the company. Without control, were liquidity to become problematic—that is, if assets became difficult to convert into cash—the company's investors might be able to take control (as once happened to the unfortunate Gutenberg when his financier took over his printing press). I did not ever want to have to answer to any lender for either my decisions or my survival.

Besides our public listing, this period also saw Pagurian's first really big investment outside of publishing. It was so successful, that it became the trigger for Pagurian's extraordinary expansion in the 1980s. That is why, in addition to going public, I say that 1979-80 was the pivotal period for Pagurian.

Black Photo, the target of Pagurian's new spending, fitted all of my criteria for a good investment, as set out by Getty and indeed, prior to his book, by Benjamin Graham and David Dodd in their standard work *Security Analysis* (a book written in 1934 in response to the great crash of 1929), which was another of my investment bibles. (Its investment philosophy could be summarized as: buy undervalued stocks, do not use debt, and bank on the long-term.) Black Photo was a company operating in the photo-finishing and photo-supply business with its own proprietary stores, a mail-order division and the ability to sell through independent markets. It was one of the dominant players in a large

*Benjamin Graham co-authored (with David Dodd) the standard work* Security Analysis *in 1934 as a response to the great crash of 1929. It is still regarded as the best book of investment philosophy ever published.*

market with a clearly defined future. It had excellent management, and over the previous five years the company had shown impressive growth in both its value and its earnings per share (a company's net profit divided by the number of its ordinary shares outstanding). But what most attracted me to Black Photo was the fact that its shares were selling at a price far below their liquid asset value as I calculated it—a classic example of what Graham and Dodd term a "good value" stock. When I first began to buy Black's shares in 1978, they were trading at three dollars and 50 cents, but according to my detailed research into the company, each share appeared to be worth almost eleven dollars in cash—three times its trading price. In other words, in Black Photo, Pagurian had a golden opportunity to buy shares for a great deal less than they were really worth.

I had no intention of interfering with the management of Black Photo. Our stake in the company was a passive investment. My plan was simply to use Pagurian's money to buy the paper issued by another company on the open market—paper that in my informed judgement would greatly increase in value over a short space of time. This continued to be my policy as Pagurian expanded in the 1980s. I never gave companies advice about managing, nor did I have any desire to. Paper and finance, not production processes and workers, were what really interested me. My task was to identify talented managers and entrepreneurs who had the capability to be highly successful, and buy into these well-run but undervalued businesses that generated a lot of cash. Then Pagurian could sit tight, let the management of the business do what it did best, and watch the value of Pagurian's minority shareholding rise. In general, our aim at that time was not to control other companies but rather to encourage good management and so share in a company's success.

In 1979, I bought a large block of shares in Black Photo, which represented eleven per cent of the outstanding value. Pagurian had now spent nearly five million dollars on Black's shares and owned 29 per cent of the company. Under Canadian accounting rules, a corporation which owns 20 per cent or more of another company can 'equity account' the earnings from that investment, provided that it can show that the company has had a significant influence on the affairs of the corporation. This meant that Pagurian could include 29 per cent of Black Photo's earnings in its annual reported net earnings. A third of Pagurian's net earnings in its 1979 accounts therefore came from Black Photo. Since stock markets tend to value companies on the basis of their earnings, our increased earnings from equity accounting helped to increase the market value of Pagurian's shares.

The following year, 1980, Pagurian's new public prominence enabled the company to issue 1.2 million class A treasury shares at eight dollars a share, with a total value of $9.6 million. The purchasers were not existing shareholders but financial institutions in France (introduced to Pagurian through our LOM office in Paris). The end result of this private placement was that the number of shares outstanding in Pagurian increased by 30 per cent, an important development because it enabled me to expand the

company's range of investors (while still retaining full control). I made it clear to the new investors that there would be further treasury share issues, both to increase the capital of the company and because I had other ambitious and hopefully profitable plans for its expansion. In 1979–80, the newly listed Pagurian was still a relatively small public company, but in the 1980s, with its increased capital, what was once a small publishing company would acquire a far more confident profile.

After the private placement, Pagurian not only increased its stake in Black Photo to 31.5 per cent (which again accounted for about a third of Pagurian's net profit in 1980), it also announced a deal to expand its investment programme into the petroleum and natural gas industry. In partnership with John Fleming, the president of the very successful company Bonanza Oil and Gas Limited, Pagurian launched a subsidiary company Westdale Oil and Gas Limited. Over the next four months, Pagurian's share price soared and reached over thirteen dollars per share.

In this heady atmosphere, in late 1980 I announced a two for one stock split, and called for a special shareholders' meeting to approve a rights issue (something I had first encountered while keeping records of the Bell Telephone rights issue in the cage at Burns Brothers). Pagurian's planned rights issue gave shareholders the right to subscribe for one unit—consisting of one subdivided class A share and one 'free' warrant to purchase a subdivided class A share—for every three subdivided class A and class B shares held by a shareholder. The subscription price for the units was $6.25 per unit; while the warrants would be exercisable at $8.50 per subdivided share until 31 December 1981, at $9.50 per share until the end of 1982 and at $10.50 per share until the end of 1983, after which the warrants would expire.

If all of the rights were taken up, I publicly and confidently announced,

*In its first decade, Pagurian maintained a positive cash flow from book publishing—a vital ingredient in its financial success. Ed Franklin (Toronto* Globe and Mail*) drew this cartoon in 1977.*

the total issue would net Pagurian funds of over $20 million, which the company was earmarking for expansion in the United States and in Europe. As for the warrants, I knew that their attraction for the company was twofold. First, they would encourage shareholders to stay invested, and secondly, they would, in all likelihood, provide a major new source of funds two or three years down the road. Obviously, I knew that the attraction for the shareholders was somewhat different. Once the rights issue was approved by the shareholders' meeting, I expected some shareholders to sell their rights, and some others to subscribe for the new units and then sell either the new shares or their warrants. But most of the shareholders, I anticipated, taking note of Pagurian's past performance and its new financing, would decide to subscribe for units and hold on to the warrants as a speculative piece of paper, hoping for much larger profits. In the event, I guessed right: most of the warrants were not exercised until the final date, at the end of 1983. Our rights issue was a well thought-out strategy in the paper game. But of course it only worked to the company's advantage because Pagurian continued to grow significantly in the three years after the rights issue.

Paper was issued, and wealth was created—it was a phenomenon; one that still excites me. Critics may call it conjuring value out of thin air—Pagurian would later on be attacked for this by some Canadian financial commentators—and it can certainly lead to destructive bubbles and crashes when it is abused (as we shall see in chapter six); but paper finance is undoubtedly what has made capitalism work effectively. Both in the era of the East India Company, and in the more complex late twentieth-century business environment.

In 1981, I felt we had realized the best part of the gain in Black Photo's share price, so I began to sell their shares and by 1982 had sold the entire holding. You never go broke taking profits—one of my top ten tips. As a rule, I have almost always sold stock early rather than sought the highest possible price. Pagurian's profitable purchase and sale of Black Photo shares in 1978–82 transformed the company—a fact that did not go unnoticed on Bay Street and had a material impact on Pagurian's share price and asset value.

However in order for Pagurian's expansion to continue, I sensed that there had to be a change in our investment policy. My judgement in investing in Black Photo in 1978–80 had been sound, with our shareholders' equity doubling each year from $13 million in 1979 to $26 million in 1980 to $55 million in 1981, largely as a result of the Black's earnings. But I had also been fortunate. It had been a passive investment in an undervalued company, which had plainly paid off for Pagurian; but it had occurred at a time when the stock market was falling due to high interest rates and shares had in general been depressed, with trading occurring in a relatively narrow price range. When the market reached bottom in 1982, I anticipated that trading would break out of this narrow range as share prices generally rose. It would then be increasingly difficult to find undervalued companies like Black's with the potential for a profitable passive investment.

A more active financial role for Pagurian was needed. Having more or less got out of publishing (except for fine art), I decided that the company must now turn itself from a modestly successful corporate investment company into a highly successful corporate finance company. Once we had established sufficient 'clout' with our reputation for success, we would be able to issue our own paper, create and finance new companies and then sell them, and through doing so profit handsomely. In the process, the company would expand from its existing sphere into a larger sphere and then into a still larger sphere—somewhat like the shell-trading hermit crab after which it was originally named.

By and large, with some hiccups, this was what actually happened. Between 1981 and 1988, when I sold Pagurian, the company virtually stopped its passive investment strategy and created its own paper in new companies. There were many of them, such as American Resource Corporation and Enfield Corporation, and Pagurian grew fast and furiously. But although its activities may sometimes have appeared complicated—as its critics were only too keen to observe—the underlying focus and operating strategies remained relatively straightforward.

Pagurian's growth as a corporate finance company was founded on the following singular and deliberate approach. First, an investment was made in the ordinary equity of a new company with attractive growth potential, which had been formed and controlled by Pagurian. This initial investment was usually reinforced with convertible preferred shares, providing the new company with cash to pursue its objectives and Pagurian with an immediate return through dividends. The second stage was to capitalize the investment by having the new company raise additional capital from either public or private markets. Finally, as the investment matured, Pagurian could derive substantial gains from selling all or part of the original investment or by allowing it to continue to grow. This process provided Pagurian with a diverse earnings stream that included dividends and equity earnings, capital gains from capitalizing longer-term investments, and, lastly, gains from the sale of mature investments. Having established a broadly based and growing earnings stream, Pagurian's results were no longer dependent on any one holding or development.

During 1981, I therefore began looking for industries with significant growth potential and the opportunity for a new company to participate in that growth. The oil and gas industry appeared ideal for Pagurian's initial venture into corporate finance—at least at first sight.

The Middle East oil price shocks of the 1970s had made the oil fields of western Canada much more attractive to the United States. The Canadian oil industry was already more than half controlled by American money, and US oil companies now prepared themselves to exploit this fact. But the Liberal Canadian government of Pierre Trudeau reacted by introducing new legislation heavily taxing potential windfall profits so as to inhibit US companies from repatriating them to the US rather than reinvesting them in Canada. The result, after some outrage in the US, was a flurry of sales of American petroleum assets and entire oil companies to Canadian companies, financed by Canadian banks. The outflow of Canadian dollars to American sellers was so massive that it weakened the Canadian currency, not to speak of the oil industry itself (although this weakness would not become apparent until the late 1980s with, most notably, the bankruptcy of Dome Petroleum).

I did not want Pagurian to be left behind. That was why we had started Westdale Oil and Gas, our joint venture with John Fleming, and taken the company public in 1980, thereby boosting Pagurian's share price so dramatically. On the other hand, I was cautious about the industry, because I knew very well that oilmen talked a language different from mine; that there was a lot of froth in the market for oil and gas stocks; and that there were also many charlatans out for a fast dollar. I would travel to Calgary in western Canada to talk to various players so as to broaden my education about the oil patch, and every time I left Calgary, I would count my fingers. After a few such trips, I realized I did not know how to make money in the oil and gas industry without taking an unreasonable amount of risk, so I began to groom the Westdale investment for sale. Part of it was later sold to Pagurian's affiliated company, Enfield, and in the end no money was lost by Pagurian. But by 1982, I had to accept that oil and gas had turned out to be a blind alley for us.

That year, the same year in which the stock market bottomed out, was the only year in Pagurian's history up to 1988 in which the company's earnings actually declined—mainly because I could not match the enormous realized gains from the sale of our shares in Black Photo the previous year. Even so, shareholders' equity again increased, and for the first time we established an annual dividend. I had not forgotten Graham and Dodd's (and Getty's) principle that successful companies should pay regular dividends. Moreover I wanted to send a strong message to the stock market that Pagurian expected better times just around the corner.

They were not too long in coming. During 1983, I was able to make an investment that epitomized my new strategy for growth. To pull off this labyrinthine deal—and in one go to nearly double Pagurian's income and vastly increase its assets—felt like throwing six balls up in the air together and making all six land in one pocket.

The deal came about as result of the manager of LOM's Geneva office introducing me to his former wife Christina Patino, whose father was Don Antenor Patino of the Bolivian mining company. Her father had just died and we knew that among the assets of his estate was a very valuable piece of paper: his ownership of 35 per cent of Edper Holdings. Edper was the holding company for Edward and Peter Bronfman—hence the name Edper—who were two brothers controlling a business empire in Toronto (cousins of the Bronfman family of Seagram and Company).

The 35 per cent block of shares was divided equally into three, between Don Antenor Patino's second wife, Beatriz, his daughter Christina and the daughter of Christina's sister, Isabelle, (who before her death had been married to the notorious financier James Goldsmith). All three wanted to sell their Edper holdings. The Bronfman brothers wanted to buy the Patino stake back. The stumbling-blocks to a sale were: first, that the Edper investment was a passive one and the assets were very illiquid, and so the Bronfmans were not willing to pay their full value in cash to the Patinos; and secondly, that the three Patino siblings hardly spoke to one another and lived on three different continents. But although I could see that forging an agreement was going to be difficult and time consuming, I persisted, because I could picture a way out of the labyrinth that would give all parties, including Pagurian, what they wanted.

After much negotiating and jetting back and forth, having argued for the illiquid nature of the assets, I managed to convince the three Patinos to agree to a sale price of $75 million. This price was at some discount to asset value, and I believed that in the right hands, the assets would be worth more than this. As with the ownership of Harlequin, which was worth more to *The Toronto Star* in 1975 than it was in the market place, again I realised that the ownership of the Edper stock would be worth more to one particular company than to any other. That company was

Hees International, the most important and profitable merchant banking operation in Canada, with ownership of natural resources and real estate (unlike Pagurian), which was itself a powerful arm of the Bronfman group of companies. The Bronfmans did not want the 35 per cent block badly enough to pay $75 million in cash for it, and neither would its banking arm Hees International, I knew that, but—here was the solution that cut the Gordian knot—Pagurian wanted to be involved with Hees. I knew that Hees was a good investment, with diverse investments complementary to Pagurian's, and I guessed that their shares would rise, if Hees could somehow acquire the Patinos' block of Edper shares on behalf of the Bronfman brothers. Pagurian could be the conduit for this sale.

I therefore decided that if Pagurian were able to cut an appropriate deal with Hees, with the simultaneous agreement of Edper's controlling shareholders (the Bronfman brothers), then Pagurian itself would buy the 35 per cent block from the Patinos for $75 million in cash and resell it to Hees in exchange for Hees treasury shares plus a smaller amount of cash. For this to happen, the six parties who had to be brought to the table, so to speak, were: the three Patinos, Edper Holdings, Hees International and Pagurian, the middleman in the negotiations.

*Jack Cockwell of Hees International and Brookfield Asset Management is one of the smartest financial men I have ever met, an investor with a long horizon, maybe 15 years; not many financiers have that much patience.*

Hees International was then run by Trevor Eaton, Jack Cockwell and Tim Price, brilliant strategists and some of the most powerful men on Bay Street. Hees was doing in corporate finance what Pagurian was doing, only with a touch more sophistication than Pagurian. Cockwell, in particular, was the smartest of all the financial men I have ever met, an investor with a long horizon, maybe 15 years; not many financiers have that much patience. In my discussions with Cockwell it became obvious that my original hunch had been right: the Patinos' Edper shares were a better buy for Hees than for Pagurian. The question was: on what terms would the company be interested in buying them? The deal I had in mind, as I explained to Cockwell, was that I intended to borrow the cash for Pagurian to buy the Edper shares, then I would exchange the Edper shares for shares in Hees and $30 million in cash. Jack agreed, valuing the Edper shares at $90 million, the price they were worth to Hees, which was $15 million more than Pagurian was going pay for them. In exchange for these Edper shares, Pagurian would receive four million ordinary shares in Hees valued at $15 each and $30 million in funds provided by the Bronfman brothers, who had agreed to buy two million Hees treasury shares, also at $15 each, from their subsidiary company.

This left me with the need to raise $75 million in cash to buy out the Patinos, which was a lot more cash than Pagurian could find in late 1983. So I went to Robert W. Korthals, president of the Toronto Dominion Bank, whom I had known in Montreal in the early 1960s, and explained the situation. I asked him for a short-term loan and when he agreed to lend Pagurian the money, I went ahead and bought the shares from the Patinos for $75 million. Although my business philosophy is not to borrow, very occasionally, if the risk is low and the opportunity is great, the rule should be broken. In this case, even though the amount of borrowing was large, I knew that it would not last for long and that it was almost certain to result in a sizeable gain. In fact, Pagurian cleared the debt within a month: I used the $30 million cash from Hees to repay the bank, and the remaining $45 million of debt was repaid largely from the sale of other Pagurian assets. Thus by early 1984, our balance sheet was clean, with no debt; we had created a good record, with considerable positive financial press coverage; and Pagurian now owned a valuable 20 per cent of Hees International. With perseverance, Pagurian's corporate financial clout had been successfully used to create a major new profitable investment. (LOM benefited too, by receiving a million-dollar commission from Pagurian and the Patinos.)

At the time of signing the deal with Hees, their shares were trading at under $15. Once Hees had acquired the Patinos' 35-per-cent holding in Edper, its parent company, the Hees share price rose—just as I had predicted it would when I embarked on the deal. Hees shares went up from $15 to $17, then $20—a substantial increase on the price at which Pagurian had acquired them. Although the deal had been difficult and had taken nine months to complete, in the end everyone had benefited. It gave the Patinos liquidity, and it cemented a profitable relationship between Pagurian and Hees. The close understanding that developed between Pagurian and Hees management after 1983 would pave the way for my eventual sale of Pagurian to Hees in 1988.

At the time, however, the idea of such a sale was very far from my mind. The three years or so, 1984–87, beginning with our deal with Hees International, were dazzling years for Pagurian, in which our assets took off in leaps and bounds through the calculated issuing of paper. It would be tedious and unprofitable for the reader if I were to describe every major investment, successful or otherwise. Suffice it to say, that Pagurian continued to invest in other companies and to create new companies, notably Enfield in 1984 and Canadian Express in 1985, in conjunction with partners, and International Pagurian in 1986; and that we expanded our operations in Europe. I personally spent much of this time living and working in England, where I bought a flat overlooking Sloane Square in London and a Victorian country house in Devon not far from my old school. Although Canada had been very good to me, and the heart of Pagurian's business was in Canada, I increasingly felt that its future, if it were to go on growing, would have to be international. To do this, I would have to make England my base.

By 1986–87, Pagurian had become a 'glamour stock', as had happened with Velcro stock in the late 1960s, and our share price rose to a record high of $19 in 1987 (from six dollars in 1984). The cover of the company's annual report for 1985, instead of a Pagurian-owned historical painting or an early map of Canada, carried a photo of one of our directors, the Norwegian financier and mountaineer Arne Naess, standing on the summit of Mount Everest, wearing an oxygen mask and reading a Pagurian annual report. (Pagurian had been one of the expedition's sponsors.) Naess showed a film of his climb at our annual meeting in 1986, from where *The Financial Post* reported with some excitement:

> As President Christopher Ondaatje was about to launch into his welcoming speech, a tall woman in an ankle-length yellow and black ensemble and wild mane of hair whooshed into the quiet room and up to a seat in the front row.
>
> A ripple ran through the crowd as some of the older

*Diana Ross (left) arrived late, just in time for the opening of the 1986 Pagurian Corporation annual meeting.*

*Arne Naess (right), eventually the husband of Diana Ross, on the summit of Mount Everest with a copy of the 1985 Pagurian annual report.*

shareholders asked their seat neighbours who she was. Whether or not they were familiar with the music of singer Diana Ross, they seemed to perk up at the news that a famous entertainer was in their midst.

Ross is married to Arne Naess, Norwegian financier and, as of last week, director of Pagurian. Naess is head of Naess Europe Ltd, an investment company run out of London. Ondaatje hopes his expertise will be helpful in developing Pagurian's newest investment—50-per-cent-owned Canadian Express—with which he hopes to carve a foothold in the international financial arena.

I was hugely enjoying myself, receiving adulation (and its inevitable opposite) and making a great deal of money for Pagurian—beyond my wildest imaginings. But I was not deceived by this success. I have always thought that if something looks too good to be true—it usually is (another of my ten tips). During 1986 and the early part of 1987, I ignored the frenzy around our company and got liquid, forgoing many

profit opportunities. The formation of International Pagurian was part of this master plan. I had the feeling that there was trouble ahead in the markets, and if our assets were not in cash or very senior securities, I would not have the option to sell the company if I wanted to.

In early 1987, as the share price of Pagurian peaked at $19, the stock markets, which had performed phenomenally, soaring to ever-increasing heights since their low in 1982, started to become unsettled. The storm clouds on the horizon told me that it was going to become more difficult to keep building Pagurian by financing new companies. Either I would have to change direction to protect the value of the company, or I would have to sell it. Postponing a definite decision, I nevertheless began to shift more valuable investments into International Pagurian, taking back convertible preferred shares in exchange and raising new equity financings in the new company. This produced a clean balance sheet, which would make the company easier and perhaps more tax efficient to sell, if and when the time became ripe to do so.

In October 1987, the worldwide stock-market collapse occurred, and in a sense the decision was made for me. Pagurian's share price collapsed in the market massacre and fell to below ten dollars, though it recovered somewhat in the following year. It was obvious to me that to issue new paper in the market place would now be almost impossible for Pagurian. There was pressure on me from investors and shareholders to continue to expand earnings and dividends at the dizzy pace of the mid-1980s— hungry shareholders expected the return on their investments somehow to continue doubling every year. It was not difficult to realize that the particular corporate finance strategy we had employed since 1982 was not going to work any more, at least for some time to come. In this mood of self-doubt, there were two possibilities: do nothing and sit tight, or take the money and get out. As I really did not want to be sitting tight for years, I decided to sell. This was a lonely decision. But then making money is a lonely business.

Throughout 1988, I resisted making any further Pagurian investments except in short-term notes, and expanded International Pagurian's equity and financial base. Pagurian itself was now a very liquid company and a perfect target for a takeover, except that I controlled over 80 per cent of the votes. It was at this point, of maximum liquidity, that I offered the management of Hees the joint management of Pagurian, with no financial outlay for them, merely an exchange of shares (as in 1983). Having control of Pagurian's assets and being cash-rich I wanted to make my offer as attractive as possible and, if possible, irresistible. The sale of Pagurian to Hees was a perfect illustration of yet another of my top ten tips: "All I want is an unfair advantage." This was a negotiation that only I could do. And again I relied on a 'paper' transaction. In December 1988, Hees announced that it had agreed to purchase all of Pagurian's senior preference shares and a 50 per cent interest in my investment holding and management company Canadian Corporate Services Limited, in exchange for Hees ordinary shares issued to me. Immediately after the deal was closed, Canadian Corporate Services Limited also filed a notice with the Toronto Stock Exchange of its intention to purchase up to 2.5 million class A shares of Pagurian through the facilities of the Toronto Stock Exchange. Because it was a paper deal—a share exchange with no cash involved—it was also a tax-free rollover for me. It made me one of the largest single shareholders in Hees, and I was appointed vice-chairman of the company. The takeover of Pagurian gave Hees management control of a company with liquid assets of $550 million, and further control of International Pagurian, which itself controlled another $650 million in assets.

Thus in 1988 Pagurian became part of the Edper Group of companies, led at the time by Peter Bronfman and Jack Cockwell. Pagurian ultimately became a senior company within the group and provided an important source of capital to consolidate Edper's business

*Overleaf: Statistical Review of Operations of the Pagurian Corporation Limited, 1967–1988.*

# THE PAGURIAN CORPORATION LIMITED
(and Predecessor Companies Including
Pagurian Press Limited)

## Statistical Review of Operations

### AUGUST 17, 1967 TO DECEMBER 31, 1988

| | 1967 | 1968 | 1969 | 1970 | 1971 | 1972 | 1973 | 1974 | 1975 | 1976 | 1977 |
|---|---|---|---|---|---|---|---|---|---|---|---|
| **Publishing and fine art** | | | | | | | | | | | |
| Revenue | $ 29,321 | $ 49,095 | $ 43,592 | $ 73,165 | $ 79,738 | $ 194,197 | $ 213,424 | $ 420,823 | $ 472,774 | $ 788,729 | $ 771,539 |
| Direct expenses | 24,820 | 35,773 | 22,866 | 50,043 | 54,755 | 126,600 | 141,277 | 306,323 | 371,749 | 551,123 | 572,749 |
| Gross profit | 4,501 | 13,322 | 20,726 | 23,122 | 24,983 | 67,597 | 72,147 | 114,500 | 101,025 | 237,606 | 198,790 |
| **Investments** | | | | | | | | | | | |
| Realized gains | | 5,432 | 11,583 | 21,965 | 18,726 | 12,826 | | 15,384 | 60,627 | 186,869 | 622,512 |
| Dividend and interest income | 87 | 1,034 | 1,006 | 4,818 | 4,844 | 875 | 5,139 | 28,348 | 36,883 | 143,626 | 152,202 |
| | 87 | 6,466 | 12,589 | 26,783 | 23,570 | 13,701 | 5,139 | 43,732 | 97,510 | 330,495 | 774,714 |
| Interest expense | | | 110 | 60 | 133 | | | | | 69,548 | 73,022 |
| | 87 | 6,466 | 12,479 | 26,723 | 23,437 | 13,701 | 5,139 | 43,732 | 97,510 | 260,947 | 701,692 |
| | 4,588 | 19,788 | 33,205 | 49,845 | 48,420 | 81,298 | 77,286 | 158,232 | 198,535 | 498,553 | 900,482 |
| Administrative expenses | 658 | 2,374 | 4,949 | 5,873 | 7,061 | 12,504 | 22,627 | 70,193 | 84,177 | 165,491 | 239,116 |
| | 3,930 | 17,414 | 28,256 | 43,972 | 41,359 | 68,794 | 54,659 | 88,039 | 114,358 | 333,062 | 661,366 |
| Income taxes | 1,244 | 4,700 | 6,700 | 12,300 | 8,800 | 21,777 | 14,858 | 26,606 | 35,543 | 75,230 | (12,168) |
| | 2,686 | 12,714 | 21,556 | 31,672 | 32,559 | 47,017 | 39,801 | 61,433 | 78,815 | 257,832 | 673,534 |
| **Corporate investments** | | | | | | | | | | | |
| Greywood Publishing | | | 17,078 | (4,578) | 963 | (415) | (25,631) | 5,583 | | | |
| Modern Canadian Library | | | | | | 25,973 | 39,424 | 673 | 36,706 | | |
| Black Photo Corporation | | | | | | | | | | | |
| Westdale Oil & Gas | | | | | | | | | | | |
| American Resource Corporation | | | | | | | | | | | |
| Hees International Bancorp | | | | | | | | | | | |
| Enfield Corporation | | | | | | | | | | | |
| Canadian Express (International) | | | | | | | | | | | |
| Canadian Express Limited | | | | | | | | | | | |
| **Net income** | $ 2,686 | $ 12,714 | $ 38,634 | $ 27,094 | $ 33,522 | $ 72,575 | $ 53,594 | $ 67,689 | $ 115,521 | $ 257,832 | $ 673,534 |

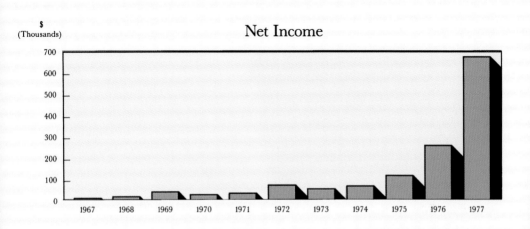

$
(Thousands)

**Net Income**

| | 1978 | 1979 | 1980 | 1981 | 1982 | 1983 | 1984 | 1985 | 1986 | 1987 | 1988 |
|---|---|---|---|---|---|---|---|---|---|---|---|
| | $ 838,038 | $ 399,286 | $ 225,156 | $ 568,423 | $ 306,519 | $ 184,748 | $ 305,592 | $ 346,080 | $ 646,198 | $ 475,030 | $1,787,302 |
| | 706,270 | 250,106 | 153,152 | 328,554 | 214,119 | 182,552 | 244,059 | 246,912 | 573,037 | 415,765 | 1,755,050 |
| | 131,768 | 149,180 | 72,004 | 239,869 | 92,400 | 2,196 | 61,533 | 99,168 | 73,161 | 59,265 | 32,252 |
| | 934,055 | 1,725,349 | 3,959,636 | 8,789,464 | 3,714,178 | 11,844,053 | 11,559,717 | 15,657,703 | 4,404,547 | 5,997,983 | 4,488,113 |
| | 346,269 | 165,630 | 730,763 | 4,149,513 | 2,958,066 | 3,450,983 | 6,114,083 | 7,367,692 | 16,421,638 | 27,064,025 | 40,739,051 |
| | 1,280,324 | 1,890,979 | 4,690,399 | 12,938,977 | 6,672,244 | 15,295,036 | 17,673,800 | 23,025,395 | 20,826,185 | 33,062,008 | 45,227,164 |
| | 130,114 | 242,940 | 435,927 | 1,000,000 | | 189,786 | 3,832,734 | 40,008 | | | |
| | 1,150,210 | 1,648,039 | 4,254,472 | 11,938,977 | 6,672,244 | 15,105,250 | 13,841,066 | 22,985,387 | 20,826,185 | 33,062,008 | 45,227,164 |
| | 1,281,978 | 1,797,219 | 4,326,476 | 12,178,846 | 6,764,644 | 15,107,446 | 13,902,599 | 23,084,555 | 20,899,346 | 33,121,273 | 45,259,416 |
| | 263,713 | 230,160 | 219,275 | 435,055 | 897,104 | 1,265,779 | 1,763,936 | 1,705,886 | 3,634,402 | 4,883,010 | 5,266,146 |
| | 1,018,265 | 1,567,059 | 4,107,201 | 11,743,791 | 5,867,540 | 13,841,667 | 12,138,663 | 21,378,669 | 17,264,944 | 28,238,263 | 39,993,270 |
| | (45,276) | 201,646 | 898,577 | 3,451,447 | 1,086,966 | 2,527,271 | 2,123,018 | 4,300,011 | 4,042,766 | 6,284,000 | 9,317,000 |
| | 1,063,541 | 1,365,413 | 3,208,624 | 8,292,344 | 4,780,574 | 11,314,396 | 10,015,645 | 17,078,658 | 13,222,178 | 21,954,263 | 30,676,270 |
| | | 723,632 | 1,341,417 | 152,209 | | | | | | | |
| | | | | 135,994 | 14,995 | | | | | | |
| | | | | 372,972 | 2,121,335 | 1,269,195 | 173,024 | | | | |
| | | | | | | | 11,156,000 | 7,709,300 | 13,535,650 | 14,760,000 | 55,945,000 |
| | | | | | | | 452,000 | 3,487,974 | 20,249,785 | 51,500,000 | |
| | | | | | | | | 525,000 | 1,880,050 | | |
| | | | | | | | | | 15,985,344 | 245,000 | 2,550,000 |
| | $1,063,541 | $2,089,045 | $4,550,041 | $8,953,519 | $6,916,904 | $12,583,591 | $21,796,669 | $28,800,932 | $64,873,007 | $88,459,263 | $89,171,270 |

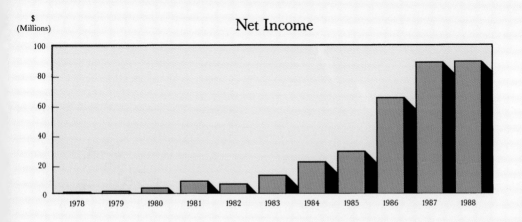

$
(Millions)

## Net Income

operations. Over time, as the ownership of the group became stream-lined, several other major companies were amalgamated into Pagurian to form Brookfield Asset Management Inc., an asset management company with a current market capitalization of US$17 billion. Shareholders of Pagurian have benefited from the stewardship of the Brookfield management team: one Pagurian share that was quoted at $8.50 at the end of 1988 has a value in equivalent Brookfield shares of more than $50.00 at the time of writing; they have also received generous annual dividend payments throughout this period. Those shareholders who have had the patience to stick with the new managers have done very well in the years since the 1988 sale.

I had built a financial empire of paper—and then I had voluntarily let it go. I had capitalised every thing I had done over the previous 22 years, and I had made more money than I had ever dreamed possible. But I was tired of the pressure, and I really did want to do something else. It was as clear to me then, as it is now, that there is much more to life than simply making money, as I admitted to *Toronto Life* in 1989 after the sale of Pagurian: "I'm *least* proud of making money, I *panic* about not doing something worthwhile with it." In 1988, I had produced another book, *Leopard in the Afternoon*—the first since *The Prime Ministers of Canada* and *Olympic Victory* in 1967—about a recent visit to Africa, and it had set me thinking about further books. I was also contemplating my first visit to Ceylon, now Sri Lanka, since leaving the island (and my father) in 1948. And I wanted to become involved in supporting institutions that really needed my assistance and know-how—such as Dalhousie University, Massey College, and Pearson College in Canada; and the National Portrait Gallery and the Royal Geographical Society in England.

But that is a different story. In the final chapter of this book, let us return to the power of financial paper, and specifically to a subject that increasingly concerns me: the abuse of paper in the global markets.

# CHAPTER 6

# *Warnings from History: The Abuse of Paper*

*Money . . . has often been a cause of the delusion of multitudes. Sober nations have all at once become desperate gamblers, and risked almost their existence upon the turn of a piece of paper. To trace the history of the most prominent of these delusions is the object of the present pages. Men, it has been well said, think in herds; it will be seen that they go mad in herds, while they only recover their senses slowly, and one by one.*

CHARLES MACKAY, preface to the second edition of
*Extraordinary Popular Delusions and the Madness of Crowds*, 1852

More than a decade after I had left the financial world, BBC Radio asked me to take part in the long-running programme *Desert Island Discs*. While I was chatting about the favourite pieces of music I would take to my imaginary desert island, the interviewer asked me why I chose to give up a lucrative career in business to do something completely different. I replied—because I did not want 'Financier' emblazoned on my gravestone.

Of course, I am scarcely the first financier to feel ambivalent about finance. Or the first financier to have left the financial world prematurely and used his money to accomplish things other than making more money, including philanthropy. But what is rather less common among former financiers who have turned to other activities is my background as a former subject of an imperial colony. My teenage exposure to Empire (both British and Dutch) in Ceylon, and the interest in history that it inculcated, shaped my business career in many ways—obvious, and not so obvious. Empire was plainly what sent me from far-away Ceylon to England to be educated, got me a job at the National Bank of India, and caused me to emigrate from England to Canada, as already described; but Empire also played a part, if more subtly, in my abandonment of corporate finance and my return from Canada to England and to Ceylon.

I wrote of my attitude to the British Empire in *Woolf in Ceylon*, a recent book of mine about the life of the successful Edwardian British imperialist Leonard Woolf who eventually became a well-known anti-imperialist, as follows: "I certainly view my colonial childhood with nostalgia for a lost age, but I take a philosophical view of the British Empire as a historical phenomenon. I regard it as the product mainly of unstoppable technological and economic trends in Europe in the 18th and 19th centuries, notably the Industrial Revolution and the accumulation of capital." I concluded: "For this reason, it does not make sense to me to say, today, that I am 'against' the British Empire. Yet it is equally clear to me that the dismantling of the British Empire was a desirable thing to have happened. There may be an element of genuine contradiction in these two attitudes of mine, but if so, it was shared by Leonard Woolf."

So how does this divided attitude to imperialism and empires relate to my ambivalence towards capitalism and its middleman, finance? In a nutshell, I deeply admire the energy, boldness and persistence that have always driven the building of great empires—whether they be the Greek, the Roman or the British Empires. I also admire the great commercial and technological achievements of modern capitalism—"an empire that is more global in its coverage than any previous empire", in the words of the financier George Soros—such as the East India Company, the Canadian-Pacific Railroad and today's global corporation Microsoft. On the other hand, I feel little admiration, in fact more like disgust, for the downside of both imperialism and capitalism, which

I have experienced at first hand: the arrogance and decadence inherent in empires, and the speculation and greed endemic in the financial world.

Alexander Pope, the 18th-century poet, put this downside of the power of paper devastatingly well in an "Epistle to Lord Bathurst" written after the collapse of the South Sea Bubble in 1720. His poem appears in the chapter devoted to the bubble in a 19th-century book still much read by financiers, Charles Mackay's *Extraordinary Popular Delusions and the Madness of Crowds*, which is where I first came across it. Pope writes:

> *At length corruption, like a general flood,*
> *So long by watchful ministers withstood,*
> *Shall deluge all; and avarice, creeping on,*
> *Spread like a low-born mist, and blot the sun;*
> *Statesman and patriot ply alike the stocks,*
> *Peeress and butler share alike the box,*
> *And judges job, and bishops bite the town,*
> *And mighty dukes pack cards for half-a-crown;*
> *See Britain sunk in Lucre's sordid charms . . .*

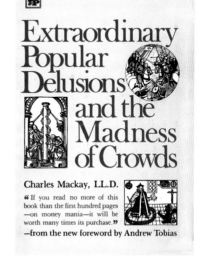

Extraordinary Popular Delusions and the Madness of Crowds, *written by Charles Mackay in 1841 is a book still much read by financiers.*

*The South Sea Bubble of 1720 satirized in an engraving by William Hogarth.*

After the South Sea Bubble imploded, a Parliamentary enquiry discovered the most flagrantly disreputable collusion between the directors of the South Sea Company and politicians of all social classes, including the Chancellor of the Exchequer himself, who was expelled from the House of Commons and imprisoned in the Tower of London in 1721. It seems to me, having watched the increasingly global empire of paper over half a century, that governments, and the modern civilization that depends on them, are once again being seduced by "lucre's sordid charms". While I am not unwise enough to prophesy what is going to happen to the world's financial system in the next few years, this final chapter of the book will discuss what I, and some others with an interest in history, consider to be dangerous warning signs.

\* \* \*

"The fate of empires"—a forthright but also nuanced essay by General Sir John Glubb that appeared in 1976—offers a number of fascinating insights into both imperial and financial history. Glubb, known as Glubb Pasha, was a British army officer who in 1939–56 commanded the Arab Legion, an army of Arab tribesmen in Transjordan and its successor state, Jordan. Glubb was therefore intimately familiar with both the British Empire in the Middle East and, as an author of books on the Middle East in later life, with the history of the Arabs and their empires.

His essay takes the long view of empires. He looks for what different empires have in common over three millennia, and he considers why this should be so.

To begin with, Glubb considers the duration of empires. He notes that their duration is not dependent on the physical extent of an empire or the speed of travel in it. For example, the relatively compact Assyrian Empire in the first millennium BC marched on foot, while the far-flung British

*Sir John Glubb's nuanced essay on "The Fate of Empires" published in 1976, offers a number of fascinating insights into both imperial and financial history.*

Empire used ships, railways and motor vehicles. Yet both empires endured for about the same length of time: the Assyrian Empire from 859–612 BC (247 years) and the British Empire from around 1700 to around 1950 (250 years). The durations of other empires—the Persian, the Greek (Alexander and his successors), the Roman, the Arab, the Mameluke, the Ottoman, the Spanish and the Romanov—persuade Glubb that empires function effectively for approximately 250 years, or ten generations of their people. However, as he frankly admits, this is only true of the Romans if their period of greatness is divided into two: the Republic (260–27 BC) and the Empire (27 BC to AD 180) up to the death of Marcus Aurelius; and he concedes that his 250-year rule does not apply to the Babylonian Empire of Nebuchadnezzar, which endured for only 74 years before its overthrow by Cyrus. Moreover, Glubb omits from his list of empires the Mongol Empire, the Aztec Empire, the Chinese Empire and the dynasties of the Egyptian pharaohs, none of which conveniently fits his proposed common duration. (The Soviet Empire, still going strong when Glubb wrote, lasted for some 70 years only.) Even so, despite several exceptions and doubts about how to define the duration of empires (which he freely shares), his suggestion of a common duration is a thought-provoking one.

This similarity in imperial rises and falls strikes Glubb as being the result of human nature. He therefore sets about dividing historical empires into 'natural' stages. The first stage is the Age of Pioneers, characterized by an outburst of initiative, enterprise, courage and aggression. The development of military forces then leads to the Age of Conquests. Initially, as the new empire becomes stronger, it is able passively to defend itself from attacks by others. Then it goes on the offensive and enters a period of conquest marked by superior organization and discipline with professional military campaigns. Acquisition of territory is vital, since larger areas of imperium are of benefit to commerce and imperial stability, whether the annexation is achieved by voluntary submission or by force. The ensuing prosperity allows the Age of Commerce to flourish, when the desire to make money, gradually, and almost imperceptibly, supersedes ideas of honour and glory gained in war. Glubb writes that, "The first direction in which wealth injures the nation is a moral one . . . . Men do not normally seek to make money for their country or their community, but for themselves. . . . The object of the young and the ambitious is no longer fame, honour or service, but cash." As an army man, Glubb's stance is not surprising, indeed he summarizes this period of growth in an empire as a move "from service to selfishness". In his scheme, the Age of Commerce inevitably yields to the Age of Affluence, in which the imperialists are preoccupied with protecting their wealth and luxuries. Money is used to buy off enemies and military interventions are deemed uncivilized— a public position that, according to Glubb, has nothing to do with conscience and much to do with an increase in selfishness among the wealthy.

The surplus of wealth allows empires to enter their penultimate stage, the Age of Intellect, where funds are freely available for education. Fame and prestige are sought through patronage of the arts and academic excellence. Instead of military action, the Age of Intellect is dominated by endless discussion and debate and, consequently, an incompetence in public affairs: "Amid a Babel of talk, the ship drifts onto the rocks." Survival of an empire depends on the loyalty and self-sacrifice of the citizens; the intellect on its own cannot solve political problems.

Ultimately, says Glubb, the empire arrives at the Age of Decadence, marked by cynicism, frivolity and a weakening of religion. "The citizens . . . will no longer make an effort to save themselves, because they are not convinced that anything in life is worth saving." In this atmosphere, the heroes of the hour are athletes, singers and actors. "The word 'celebrity' today is used to designate a comedian or a football player, not a states-man, a general, or a literary genius." (In late 10th-century Baghdad, adds Glubb with some relish, several Caliphs issued orders banning sexually suggestive 'pop' singers from the capital, but within a few years they always returned.) Decadence is the result of too long a period of wealth and power, leading to selfishness, a love of money and the loss of a sense of duty. Glubb states that history proves empires are in decline when they become philanthropic, for example by spending on a welfare state. They overspend, because there is an assumption that they will always be rich, progress will be automatic, and wealth will be attained with minimal effort. Economic collapse eventually ensues, although the precise reasons for the fall of an empire often involve diverse external factors.

In summing up his thesis, Glubb writes: "We have not drawn from history the obvious conclusion that material success is the result of courage, endurance and hard work."

Glubb's arguments were undoubtedly over-influenced by his lifelong immersion in the history of the Arabs, and probably influenced, too, by the humiliating state of the British economy in 1976 (the date of his essay), which had to be salvaged in that year with a massive loan from the International Monetary Fund. But Glubb's ages of empire still seem to me to be worth considering in relation to today's dominant empire. I do not mean the United States, but rather the global capitalist system. As George Soros remarked in his millennial book, *Open Society: Reforming Global Capitalism*:

> The empire analogy is apt because the global capitalist system governs those who belong to it—and it is not easy to opt out. Moreover, it has a centre and a periphery like every empire, the centre benefiting at the expense of the periphery. Most important, global capitalism exhibits expansionist tendencies. Far from seeking equilibrium, it is hell-bent on conquest. It cannot rest as long as there are markets and resources that remain unincorporated into the system. . . . Despite its non-territorial nature, the system does have a centre and a periphery. Although the exact location of the centre is nebulous, for practical purposes it is identified with

the United States and to a lesser extent with Europe, and
Japan is poised somewhere between centre and periphery.
The centre is the provider of capital; the periphery is the
user of capital.

If we accept the analogy between global capitalism and empire, then it
seems plausible to associate Glubb's Age of Pioneers with the seventeenth
century, when the East India companies started to explore and trade; the
Age of Conquests with the eighteenth century, when the British Empire
came into being; and the Age of Commerce with most of the nineteenth
century. In this latter period, the economy was dominated by the gold
standard, the liberalization of trade and the growth in industrialization,
which combined to produce the first phase of globalization. Although
Britannia ruled the waves, many other countries, particularly those in
Europe, benefited from the free flow of capital, labour and goods.

The next stage, the Age of Affluence of the global capitalist empire,
could be associated with the steep growth in limited-liability companies,
stock markets and other paper investments, during the final decades
of the nineteenth century and the early decades of the twentieth century,
ending with the depression of the 1930s. Between the two world wars
there was economic strife but only a brief lull in the development
of globalization. Following the Second World War, the International
Monetary Fund, the World Bank and the General Agreement on Tariffs
and Trade came into existence. Global capitalism might be said to
have now entered the Age of Intellect, with mass higher education and
continual discussion, debate, protest and counter-protest leading to badly
managed public affairs. If so, then the question is, what of the Age of
Decadence? When does that begin for global capitalism? If we follow
Glubb's 250-year rule, and make the reasonable assumption that the
beginning of this latest of empires must lie somewhere in the period
1750–1850, then it is at least possible that we are now in the Age of
Decadence.

The recent moves to drop Africa's debt to Western countries and the pressure on the G8 group of industrialized nations to implement restrictions on free-market trading, not to speak of the seemingly endless 'reforms' of Britain's National Health Service—could be read as the symptoms of an empire beginning to wallow in decadence. But since I am a financier by training, not an economist or a politician, I shall restrict myself to the paper manifestations of possible decadence.

The production and prevalence of paper in the global financial system accelerated during the twentieth century, and its proliferation has particularly increased during the last 30 years. This is true of both banknotes and other financial instruments, such as bonds and shares, used to create credit. There are now fourteen billion paper US dollars in existence, a third of which are held outside the United States; dollar bills are more numerous than any other branded object, including Coke cans. In order to understand how this paper world has materialized and what its implications might be, it is worth going back to the operation of the gold standard as a comparison.

The gold standard meant that anyone could literally demand payment in gold from the Bank of England in exchange for its banknotes. The gold standard fixed the value of a country's currency as based on its gold reserves, thereby setting the exchange rates between the currencies of different countries. From the nineteenth century until the early 1930s, it was supposed to ensure a balance in international trade, in accordance with the ideas of classical economists (such as Ricardo) who believed that such a balance between imports and exports was necessary for a sustainable national economy. The magic of the gold standard was that it created a self-correcting economic mechanism. A country that succeeded too well in exporting goods would eventually be faced with an excess of gold. This would create credit, and credit would cause price inflation in the country. In turn, inflation would reduce the country's export competitiveness, as trading partners looked to other countries for cheaper goods. Exports would therefore decline, imports would rise and gold would flow out of the country. With the drain in gold, credit would contract, a recession would prompt a fall in prices, which would once again stimulate trade competitiveness—and the cycle would begin again.

Britain did not come off the gold standard until the beginning of the war in 1914. Yet as Peter Clarke notes of the British economy in *Hope and Glory*, "Imports exceeded exports in value by well over £100 million in most years around the turn of the century." However, no one was worried because "The earnings of the City alone were sufficient to fill the payments gap in the years immediately before the First World War." Clarke refers to this as "invisible income". It was made up of paper income, generated by the City's instruments of finance, which created enforceable contracts, and money generated by overseas properties and the dominance of British shipping that had helped to create the Empire. Britain's 'unfair advantage' meant it could call the shots in the world markets. British traders, shippers, insurers and bankers, and the City of London as a whole, benefited, and in the Edwardian era, British millionaires multiplied—plutocrats whose money had been made in finance, not from industry as in the preceding century. But then the First World War crippled the British economy. In 1914, the national debt was £620 million, but by 1920 it stood at nearly £8,000 million. Britain did not return to the gold standard until 1925, but found that the debt made it unworkable, and in 1931 it abandoned the gold standard for ever.

The United States, which had been on the gold standard since 1879, followed Britain's decision two years later, and withdrew from it. However, not entirely. Gold was officially required in US bank deposits until 1968 to support a percentage of the currency in circulation. Furthermore, for transactions with overseas monetary authorities, the dollar would remain convertible into gold until 1971. The US decision to leave the gold standard in 1933 was not a result of war but of the deep depression and record unemployment following the Wall Street stock-market crash of 1929, when radical government spending programmes were called for. The theories of classical economics were rejected by the Roosevelt Administration in favour of state intervention, just as John Maynard Keynes would recommend economic intervention to the British government in the 1930s.

Franklin Roosevelt's New Deal, apart from its famous deficit funding of large-scale public works to provide employment for the legions of the unemployed, also included legislation to control the financial world. Roosevelt was shocked by the irresponsibility of Wall Street in the 1920s—epitomized by such obsessive large-scale speculators as Jesse Livermore (mentioned in chapter two)—and he was determined to regulate the stock exchanges and the paper world. Steven Fraser's recent history, *Wall Street*, quotes Roosevelt as saying in 1934: "The fundamental trouble with this whole stock exchange crowd is their complete lack of elementary education. I do not mean lack of college

*Franklin Delano Roosevelt was shocked by the irresponsibility of Wall Street in the 1920s and was determined to regulate the stock exchanges and the paper world.*

diplomas, etc., but just inability to understand the country or public or their obligations to their fellow men."

The upshot was the creation of the Securities and Exchange Commission (SEC) in 1934 to supervise stock-exchange trading, and an assumption of greater authority over the markets by the Federal Reserve, ending the self-regulation of the stock exchanges. In addition, insider trading became a crime and new corporate reporting standards were introduced.

A key piece of legislation passed by the US Congress at this time was the Glass-Steagall Act (GSA). In the 1920s, America's commercial banks had encouraged speculation by buying new issues of unsound stock and selling them to their customers against bank loans. The basic objective of the GSA was to erect a barrier between the commercial banks and the merchant banks. Commercial banks were prohibited from collaborating with brokerage firms or from participating in investment banking. A commercial bank was permitted to earn no more than ten per cent of its total income from bond issues. In effect, depositors' money in the commercial banking system would no longer be available to shore up the underwriting of new stock and bond issues, or to be invested directly in the stock market. The GSA thus targeted the heart of Wall Street, restricting the power of large new-issue dealers like the giant J. P. Morgan and Company. The Wall Street finance houses were of course furious, but despite their virulent enmity for the Roosevelt Administration, Wall Street had no political power and consequently no impact on the 1936 presidential election, in which Roosevelt was re-elected with a landslide victory. The Truman Administration that succeeded Roosevelt's in 1945 maintained the same interventionist policies, and it was not until well into the 1950s that stock prices on Wall Street regained some of their former strength. Not until 1999, under the Clinton Administration, did Wall Street finally succeed in having the GSA dismantled for being outmoded in an era of free-market competition.

On the international scene, as a result of the depression and the Second

World War, laissez-faire policies towards the world of paper finance were also out of fashion. In 1944, the United Nations conference at Bretton Woods in New Hampshire, convened to discuss post-war reconstruction, resulted in the creation of the International Monetary Fund and the World Bank. It also introduced an economic system that worked like the gold standard with a system of fixed exchange rates: the US dollar was tied to gold at $35 per ounce and all other major currencies were tied to the dollar at agreed rates. The US dollar was therefore still backed by the gold reserves of the US, and remained convertible for currency-exchange purposes with other countries.

For over 20 years, the Bretton Woods system functioned effectively, but in the late 1960s it began to collapse. Heavy US overseas investment and massive military expenditure on the Vietnam War caused the US balance of payments to deteriorate. Foreign countries were eager to exchange their dollars for gold, and in 1971 the Nixon Administration suspended convertibility to stem the flow of American gold from Fort Knox. In 1973, the Bretton Woods system was at last scrapped and currencies were allowed to float. Without fixed exchange rates, countries were free to expand without worrying about currency controls on their balance of payments. The discipline of a gold-backed currency changed to one in which the US dollar became the reserve currency of the world, with no backing except the unenforceable promise of the US government that it would honour and protect the value of its currency.

From this point on, paper finance took over the economies of the world. After 1971, the United States no longer had to pay for imports with gold or dollars backed by gold. Instead, other kinds of financial instrument could be used to create credit, such as equities, bonds and financial derivatives. The US government's reserve assets, once made of gold, are now largely made of paper. It may seem incredible that paper sustains the global economic system with nothing but other pieces of paper as security, but that is today's reality.

There has been no shortage of commentators in recent years warning of the risks inherent in this situation. The basic concern is always, what will happen if the rest of the world loses trust in the value of the dollar? Richard Duncan, in his book *The Dollar Crisis: Causes, Consequences, Cures*, published in 2003, writes bluntly that, "The creation of credit backed only by paper reserves has generated a worldwide credit bubble characterized by economic overheating and severe asset price inflation . . . . The economic house of cards built with paper dollars has begun to wobble. Its fall will once again teach the world why gold—not paper— has been the preferred store of value for thousands of years."

Alan Greenspan, Chairman of the US Federal Reserve Board from 1987 until 2006—who was described on his retirement as "the greatest economist of his generation" by the British Chancellor of the Exchequer Gordon Brown—changed his mind about gold and paper. In the 1960s, Greenspan was associated with the writer and philosopher Ayn Rand, who strongly advocated unbridled laissez-faire capitalism. In this spirit,

*In December 1996 Alan Greenspan, Chairman of the US Federal Reserve Board, coined the phrase "irrational exuberance" in an attempt to convey that the risk premiums on paper instruments were set too low.*

Greenspan wrote several articles supporting the gold standard, in which he suggested that money not backed by gold was almost fraudulent. But once he became Chairman of the 'Fed', Greenspan added $4.5 trillion to the US money supply—double the amount printed by all previous chairmen. In *Financial Reckoning Day*, another book published in 2003, William Bonner describes Greenspan as the greatest paper-money monger the world has ever seen. During his tenure in office, fiat money gained substantially in value against gold. "In 1980, it took as many as 850 dollars to buy an ounce of gold. Twenty-two years later, that very same ounce changed hands at only $280. Greenspan, formerly a gold bug, now a paper bug, must have smiled to himself," writes Bonner. But this new fiat money had no metal backing: "Paper money, like pro forma earnings, could be anything the government said it was. A valuable tool in self-delusion and deceit, paper money could also suddenly become worthless."

In the stock-market recession of 2000, after the collapse of the technology stock bubble, the Federal Reserve, ignoring any risk of inflation, responded by lowering interest rates to a level that had not been seen since the early 1950s, flooding the market with liquidity. The liquidity found its way into assets, and rescued the stock market. The technology stocks had collapsed, but the rest of the market, after the correction, roared back, and the profits found their way into housing and consumer goods.

With Greenspan in the driving seat, the financial world realized that the Federal Reserve would rather see bubbles continue than face up to a severe recession if the bubbles were tackled. The term 'Greenspan put' entered the modern lexicon. A put option in the stock market is a form of risk insurance. In exchange for a risk premium, a seller buys the right, if he chooses, to sell a piece of paper on a specified date at a specified price, thus protecting himself against a severe price decline. If the price of the paper declines below the put price on that date, the insurer must cover the difference between the put price and the lower market price paid to the seller by the buyer. The 'Greenspan put' expressed the market's assumption that the Federal Reserve would always insure the buoyancy of the stock market by cutting interest rates, so that a sour market would rise again. The effect of such federal intervention, however, was to promote the speculation of the biggest market gamblers, not the general well-being of the stock market. If one of the major institutions failed—as happened in 1998 with the high-risk hedge fund Long Term Capital Management—thereby posing a threat to the whole credit and banking system, then the Federal Reserve could be counted on to intervene. The overall effect of this policy was to allow bubbles to continue.

In December 1996, during a boom period, Greenspan made a speech to the American Enterprise Institute in Washington DC which gave rise to a further expression associated with his name:

> Clearly, sustained low inflation implies less uncertainty about the future, and lower risk premiums imply higher prices of stocks and other earning assets. We can see that in the inverse relationship exhibited by price/earnings ratios and the rate of inflation in the past. But how do we know when irrational exuberance has unduly escalated asset values, which then become subject to unexpected and prolonged contractions as they have in Japan over the past decade?

"Irrational exuberance" was Greenspan's attempt to convey that the risk premiums on paper instruments were set too low. The enthusiasm generated by rising prices was generating still more enthusiasm and encouraging market participants to take unrealistic risks.

Greenspan's comments might have gone unnoticed, had they not been immediately followed by a brief slump. Financial analysts interpreted his speech as a warning that the market was overvalued, and "irrational exuberance" became a commonplace expression in financial circles. However, losses were quickly recouped and not long after, dotcom mania took hold. After the technology stock market collapse in 2000, bumper stickers in Silicon Valley were spotted reading: "I want to be irrationally exuberant again."

The weakness in both the market and the Federal Reserve's policies became particularly apparent in 2001, when a sustained recession began in the US. Normally in a recession savings increase and consumer spending falls. But this recession has been marked by even greater borrowing and spending, as consumers apparently assume that good times are around the corner. Rather than being alarmed, Greenspan encouraged borrowing by stating that borrowing had a stabilizing influence on the economy. Instead, by the end of 2002, bankruptcies reached a new record and foreclosure rates were at a 30-year high. Easy-credit policies such as the one advocated by Greenspan can have a devastating effect.

The consumer binge in the US has created record trade deficits, particularly with Asian countries such as China, which, as a proportion of the US's GDP, have not been seen in generations. Banks have been very accommodating to consumers, who have remortgaged their homes to finance their consumption and to speculate in new housing, particularly in the large cities of California, the northeastern seaboard and Florida. This has been made possible by a Federal Reserve that has pushed interest rates exceptionally low and flooded the economy with liquidity. At the same time, the tax cuts of the Bush Administration have largely benefited high-income consumers, while transforming Federal finances from a large surplus into an enormous deficit, now being exacerbated by heavy government spending on the Iraq War and the aftermath of major hurricanes. In effect, the US government now depends on foreign governments, via its trade deficit, for its own finance. The debt is staggering. If the US economy were to develop cracks of a more severe nature, the global economy would in turn be thrown into crisis.

Computerization of the money markets has contributed to this fiscal irresponsibility. In *Financial Reckoning Day*, Bonner writes:

"In today's electronic world, a man no longer measures his wealth in stacks of paper money. It is now just 'information'. A central banker [Bonner obviously means Alan Greenspan] does not even have to turn the crank on the printing press; electronically registered zeros can be added at the speed of light. Given the ease with which new paper money is created, is it any wonder the old paper money loses its value?" Bonner thinks—as Glubb did—that such 'funny money' has created a moral hazard. Why try to save, when new money appears so effortlessly at such attractive rates?

Thus paper, not tax revenues or earned income, is fuelling record levels of US consumer debt, an overvalued stock market, a housing bubble and, not least, an aggressive foreign policy. Instead of financing its economy with domestic savings, the US is in effect eating its own capital by mortgaging the future.

Like every other technology, paper can be both beneficial and harmful. It creates credit, which can be a vital way of sustaining economic growth, but its over-production can lead to economic disaster—as first happened in China in the eleventh century. Throughout history, the over-production of banknotes has caused inflation and, eventually, economic collapse. There are real and present dangers in the current expansion of credit, in the number of dollars in circulation and in the dramatic multiplication of financial instruments.

As Bill Lucarelli writes in *Monopoly Capitalism in Crisis*, a book published in 2004, "Money is increasingly an endogenous function of private financial institutions. Credit tends to incessantly expand the limits of accumulation. With the issuing of bank money, credit supersedes the limits imposed by the level of savings. It follows that, under a finance-led regime of accumulation, crises become endemic." Lucarelli claims that between 1986 and 1996 bond issues tripled, securities issues increased by more than tenfold and foreign-exchange transactions quadrupled to over one trillion dollars. And he links this financial explosion to a decline in the power of the United States: "Just as the interwar crisis witnessed a global transition from one hegemonic power to another—or from the free trade imperialism of *Pax Britannica* to the rise of *Pax Americana* under the aegis of the post-war Bretton Woods System—so too the present systemic crisis carries with it the clash between the three great hegemonic powers of the EU, Japan/East Asia and the US."

Leaving aside governments and nations, consider the effect on ordinary consumers of their increasing dependence on the performance of the stock market—especially in the United States. This began with the growth in the institutional market after the end of the Truman years. In 1952, the economist Harry Markowitz published an essay, "Modern portfolio theory", which in 1990 earned him a Nobel Prize in economics. His theory stated that a well-chosen, diversified portfolio of shares was less risky than an individual stock, however well researched. The portfolio manager's job was to avoid 'co-variance' among a widely diversified holding of many different companies and industries. By doing so, overall risk could be minimized and returns maximized, in comparison with the least risky stock-market investment, a government bond. Intelligent portfolio management became the new holy grail for the smaller investor and as a result, the institutional market was born and grew very rapidly. (Loewen Ondaatje McCutchion was a major beneficiary in this area in Canada.)

Nonetheless, in the US in 1987, the year of the major correction in Wall Street, there were still only 25 per cent of households with a stake in the stock market. But by the late 1990s, that proportion had risen to over 50 per cent of households—invested either through mutual funds or directly in the market. In the case of mutual funds, according to the economist Robert Shiller's figures, in 1982, there were 6.2 million equity mutual-fund shareholder accounts in the United States, about one for every ten US families. By 2000, there were 164.1 million such shareholder accounts, or nearly two accounts per family. And by 2003, this figure had risen to 174.1 million accounts. All of which were invested in the stock market.

It is true that the amount invested in the market remains concentrated in relatively few hands, with 42 per cent of stocks and 56 per cent of bonds owned by the wealthiest one per cent of households. But even so, ordinary people's money is increasingly dependent on the success of the financial markets. Passive savers have been fast converted into active investors. They now have a vested interest in the performance of the markets and in the maintenance of 'neo-liberal' economic policies. Neo-liberalism supports deregulation of markets and reduction of the power of trade unions to ensure a flexible workforce, and holds that the free market will provide an efficient allocation of resources. Neo-liberalism is the general stance of many major economic institutions, including the World Bank, the International Monetary Fund and the World Trade Organization.

The growth in the number of eager smaller investors with faith in such views helped to propel the growth in varieties of financial instrument in the 1990s, such as derivatives, as financial institutions acted speedily to create new products tailored for the new investors. Everyone—from the ordinary consumer to the institutional fund manager and the corporate CEO—was keen to benefit from the stock market rises of that decade. Robert Shiller compared the atmosphere at the time to that of a gold rush in his important and thoughtful best-selling book, *Irrational Exuberance*—published in March 2000 just as the technology stock bubble quivered and burst, but before the exposure of rampant corporate corruption in companies such as Enron and WorldCom in late 2001.

During the boom years, American corporate remuneration was laced with extremely generous stock options, not only for senior management but also throughout the corporate hierarchy. Executives could expect to be rewarded with offers of their company's stock at a discount price. An option had no cost from an accounting point of view, since no money or shares changed hands until an executive exercised the option. Stock options generated an unhealthy fixation with the current stock price, and an emphasis on short-term earnings and market performance that was counterproductive to long-term corporate values. Management concentrated on appearing to excel in the short term, avoiding anything in a company's published earnings reports that could disappoint the market and thereby reduce the value of their stock options. Individual corporate executives stood to make millions of dollars if the stock price rose well above the option price, which naturally encouraged them to 'talk up' the stock and stretch the truth, or lie. They courted only those investment analysts who were partial to their company and would recommend buying its shares in their published research reports.

Executives of the international energy company Enron—which was designated "America's Most Innovative Company" for six consecutive years by *Fortune* magazine—built an entire business empire out of talk, paper and fraud, with the connivance of friendly politicians. Enron claimed revenues of $100 billion in 2000, the year before it went bankrupt. The Enron story is the story of the South Sea Company retold for our own time. After the whistle was blown by a middle-ranking employee and Enron spectacularly imploded, the well-known economist Henry Kaufman of the merchant bank Goldman Sachs admitted that Enron and many simultaneous corporate scandals encompassed all the financial excesses of the previous decade. Steve Fraser is rather more trenchant in his book *Wall Street*. Fraser says the scandals "implicated virtually the entire Wall Street banking establishment" and calls them "unprecedented looting":

> insiders making off with the accumulated assets of pension-holders and mutual-fund shareholders; book-cooking by top management designed to prop up share prices and so cash in on stock options; whole corporations that turned out to be the reincarnations of [the 1920s fraudster] Charles Ponzi's original brainstorm. Corporate insiders from the top 25 bankrupted companies made off with $3.3 billion in stock sales and bonuses as their firms went belly-up.

The US government's response to the scandals, the Sarbanes-Oxley Act (SarbOx) of 2002, addressed audits, financial reporting and disclosure, conflicts of interest and the corporate governance of public companies. It implemented supervisory mechanisms such as the Public Company Accounting Oversight Board for accountants and accounting firms that conduct external audits of public companies, so as to protect the interests of shareholders and the public from deliberate accounting inconsistencies and fraudulent practices. SarbOx requires the chief executive officer and chief financial officer of a company to certify "the appropriateness of the financial statements and disclosures contained in the [annual] report, and that those financial statements and disclosures fairly present, in all material aspects, the operations and financial condition of the issuer"; and it holds the two officers personally responsible for any violations. Non-compliance can result in criminal charges. Moreover, whistleblower protection is written into the legislation, prohibiting employers from discriminating against employees who report any violation in federal securities law.

The Sarbanes-Oxley Act (SarbOx) has been described as the most important corporate reform legislation in the US since the Securities and Exchange Act of 1934. But my own feeling is: first, that SarbOx does not go far enough, and second, that it may have come too late. Notwithstanding the increase in numbers of people investing in the stock market, too much money is now controlled by too few people. The top 100 money managers in the USA are estimated to hold 58 per cent of all US stocks. Most of these managers are passive investors. They decline to participate in company affairs, will not vote their stock at corporate meetings, and will not challenge corporate governance in public companies. This is what explains the continuing indefensible increase in executive pay scales, the overuse of stock options to reward insiders, and the unchallenged authority of management and the board of directors to manipulate the stock price of their companies.

Markets were very different in the 1950s when I began my career. As the founder and former CEO of Vanguard, one of the largest mutual funds in America, John Bogle, stated in *The Wall Street Journal* in 2005, "direct ownership of stocks by American households has declined from 91 per cent in 1950 to just 32 per cent today. The 9 per cent ownership stake held by financial institutions in 1950 crossed the 50 per cent mark in 1983, and now totals 68 per cent of all stocks. It is hard to imagine that our earlier society dominated by individual stock ownership will ever return." Then Bogle issued what amounted to a damning indictment of his own industry: "The excessive advisory fees, expenses, hefty sales loads, and huge commissions on portfolio transactions paid to brokers in return for their sales support consumed something like 45 per cent of the real returns earned on fund portfolios during the past two decades."

The stock market boom of the 1990s is now generally agreed to have led to a false sense of confidence among US investors of all kinds. What is more surprising, however, is that their confidence apparently persists, even after the stock-market correction of 2000 and the corporate scandals that followed. As Robert Shiller remarks in his new preface to the second edition of his book, published in 2005, "Irrational exuberance really is still with us."

Shiller has good reason to say this. The Bush Administration, for its own doctrinaire political reasons, likes to speak of "the ownership society", which resonates well with US voters across the political spectrum. But what this euphemism conceals is that incomes and pensions have become over-dependent on the performance of the stock market. The under-funding of US pensions is growing with the current recession. At the end of 2004, corporate America had under-funded pension liabilities estimated at over $450 billion on about $1.5 trillion in assets. "People will increasingly fear that their livelihoods really depend on their wealth, wealth that is highly unstable because of market changes," claims Shiller. In order to cope with this fact and their fears, they will therefore cling to unwarranted beliefs, such as that the market will continue to perform as it has in the recent past, that stocks will always outperform bonds, and that over time house prices will always rise. Shiller concludes soberly:

> I do not know the future, and I cannot accurately predict the ups and downs of the markets. But I do know that, despite a significant slip in confidence since 2000, people still place too much confidence in the markets and have too strong a belief that paying attention to the gyrations in their investments will someday make them rich, and so they do not make conservative preparations for possible bad outcomes.

This is the social psychology that sustains the speculative bubble. In a bubble, news of a price increase generates enthusiasm among investors, which spreads by word of mouth (and of course by email) from person to person, in the process exaggerating information that might justify the price increase and luring in an ever-expanding group of investors—who are not necessarily entirely convinced by the real value of the investment but feel a mixture of envy and excitement at taking a gamble. The longer a bubble lasts, the bigger it gets and the nastier the aftermath when it bursts. While it is growing, ethical and professional standards drop, and inappropriate loans are given for mortgages and credit. Regulatory institutions and financial commentators are to some extent won over, or at least muted by the general enthusiasm. (During the British Parliamentary debate on the South Sea Company's plan to take over the national debt, its opponent Robert Walpole, an orator who normally packed the House of Commons, spoke to deserted benches.) Bubbles are good for the economy—for a while. And there is a professional risk in speaking out against them: in the late 1990s, the market was strewn with the punctured reputations of commentators who predicted the bursting of the technology stock bubble too soon.

It is now widely accepted that the bursting of the stock market bubble in 2000 led to yet another bubble, this time in real estate, as those who had made money gambling on technology stocks found new opportunities to speculate. This is proved by Shiller's index of US house prices: from about 1950 until the late 1990s, it is fairly stable, whereas between 1997 and 2004, it increased by 52 per cent.

Mortgages are now available for 110 per cent of a house's value, lent on the assumption that real-estate prices will continue to climb; interest-only mortgages are offered, often without adequate credit checks; adjustable-rate mortgages are popular, in which the interest rate increases over time, as do the repayments. Were there to be a sudden increase in interest rates, how would many people repay their mortgages? Were the market price of the property to decline at the same time, would they elect to default? These questions are ignored. The mindset among US investors and lenders is clearly that housing prices have only one way to go—up. The housing bubble continues but, like all bubbles, the longer it grows, the worse will be the fallout when it finally bursts. The end of the housing bubble will remove a prop to the US economy that stimulated consumer spending. This could be a major deflationary shock. Because there is such widespread investment in real estate, attracting speculation from all sectors of society, when property prices eventually do go down, the impact on the US economy will be far greater than the bursting of the technology stock bubble in 2000.

I have concentrated on the stock market in the United States, because it is the world's largest. Many of its fundamental problems, such as its bubbles and its under-funding of pensions, are shared by other advanced economies, however. Even more important, the financial markets are now global, with capital increasingly free to move across national boundaries in defiance of national taxes and financial regulations—hence capitalism's equation with a global empire.

Here the leading commentator—whose analogy between global capitalism and empires was quoted earlier—is the financier George Soros, rather than the economist Shiller, whose *Irrational Exuberance* concerns

*George Soros predicted in 1998, in* The Crisis of Global Capitalism: Open Society Endangered, *that the then-current instabilities in the international financial markets would continue and capitalism would be threatened with collapse.*

primarily the US. In 1998, Soros's book, *The Crisis of Global Capitalism: Open Society Endangered*, predicted that the then-current instabilities in the international financial markets would continue and capitalism would be threatened with collapse. Two years later, he revised the book and published *Open Society: Reforming Global Capitalism*, in which he admitted he had been wrong in predicting disaster. However, the second book still foresees trouble ahead.

Soros's chief concern is more political than strictly financial. He sees an incompatibility between a global economy (which made him fabulously wealthy through international currency speculation) and a political system that is still rooted in national sovereignty. Soros warns that if we care about universal principles such as freedom and democracy, we must establish institutions to safeguard them—free-market capitalism will not guarantee them for us. Indeed, since national governments depend on capital to generate national wealth, governments have a tendency to put the needs of capital ahead of freedom, human rights and the environment.

Moreover, Soros says, the centre of the global capitalist empire will always look after itself more than its periphery. The major capitalist countries recovered well from the international financial crisis of 1997–99, but peripheral countries, notably in East Asia, suffered a depression like that of the United States in the 1930s. Indonesia's GDP fell by 15 per cent in 1998, leading to sharp falls in real incomes and employment, pushing an estimated 17 million more Indonesians below the poverty line, defined as an income of one US dollar a day. This widening gap between centre and periphery is an obvious source of social and political instability, leading to violence, as it has been in every previous empire.

As for the ability of free markets to self-correct, supposedly demonstrated in 1997–99, Soros is not convinced. He is not a 'market fundamentalist' who believes in laissez-faire at all costs: that any form of collective action will distort the performance of the markets. Market fundamentalists regard the power of the market's invisible hand as almost magical. Soros points to the danger in this: "The belief that the system will always right itself is a self-defeating prophecy. The system *did* right itself, and I was wrong when I predicted its imminent demise, but it was saved by the actions of financial authorities in response to imminent danger. Market fundamentalism could undermine the resolve of the authorities to intervene in case of need." Rather than diminishing the role of international institutions such as the International Monetary Fund, as favoured by market fundamentalists, Soros recommends the opposite: strengthening the IMF as part of the global empire's duty to prevent, rather than manage, international financial crises. Although markets are inherently unstable, that does not mean they should be left to do what they will. While Soros is certainly in favour of keeping capitalism, he believes in trying to improve its operation.

Soros was more optimistic about the future of capitalism in his second book than in his first. But he admits that the non-monetary values that give empires and civilizations their strength and endurance have increasingly been usurped by money, which rules people's lives as never before. I cannot help feeling that his optimism, like his earlier pessimism, is misplaced. In my view, an empire is on its way out, once love of money triumphs over all else.

The world economy is now based on the power of paper—but paper is not the cause of its problems. Human psychology is. The get-rich-quick mentality. Irrational exuberance. Lucre's sordid charms. Call avarice what you like. As Sir John Glubb said in "The fate of empires"—already quoted but worth repeating—"We have not drawn from history the obvious conclusion that material success is the result of courage, endurance and hard work."

History repeats itself—especially in the financial world. The foundations of the empire of global capitalism are now paper thin, and seem destined to fall causing untold chaos and confusion, not just in the western world but across the entire globe from America to China.

# SOURCES OF QUOTATIONS

## CHAPTER 1 · RICHES FROM RAGS

p. 31     "which included a large literature" Bell: 98.

p. 32     "Administrators and merchants" Robinson: 11.

p. 32     "Writing was devised" Potts, "Before Alexandria: libraries in the Ancient Near East" in MacLeod: 20.

p. 38     "It was an axiom of Alexander" MacLeod: 3.

p. 38     "an act which set a fashion" Ibid: 1.

p. 39     "This brought about the wide distribution" Collins: 5.

p. 39     "It is noteworthy" Barnes, "Cloistered book-worms in the chicken-coop of the Muses: the ancient library of Alexandria" in MacLeod: 76.

p. 42     "true negotiability" Goetzmann and Rouwenhorst: 7.

p. 43     "In contrast to Western monetary thought" Von Glahn, "The origins of paper money in China" in Goetzmann and Rouwenhorst: 66.

p. 45     "The story of Cai Lun" Bloom: 32, 45.

p. 46     "a veritable explosion" Ibid: 111.

p. 47     "financial procedure in the medieval Islamic lands" Ibid: 141.

p. 48     "Paper production served the needs" Eisenstein: 18.

p. 48     "Gutenberg's invention made" Man: 2.

p. 50     "He emerges as that rarity" Ibid: 52.

p. 52     "It is perhaps the case that a book" Febvre: 288.

p. 53     "Printing required favourable social" Briggs and Burke: 16.

p. 55     "a printer at war" Deacon: 113.

p. 56     "though Caxton dealt entirely" Ibid: 150.

p. 57     "a humanistic scholar" Warner: 3.

p. 57     "The signing of petitions" Briggs and Burke: 34.

p. 58     "Newspapers contributed to the rise" Ibid: 72.

## CHAPTER 2 · FINANCIAL INSTRUMENTS

p. 61     "Put a financial engineer" Goetzmann and Rouwenhorst: 4.

p. 61     "At some point he gave me" Ondaatje, *Fool's Gold*: 14.

p. 63     "Economics is a science" Robbins: 16.

p. 66     "trade flourished" Backhouse: 14–15.

p. 66     "Though he saw a role for trade" Ibid: 18.

p. 68     "The just price" Ibid: 45.

p. 70     "in the novel mechanism" Goetzmann and Rouwenhorst: 14.

p. 71     "Mun's theory" Backhouse: 79.

p. 74     "it was gold and silver" Ibid: 87.

p. 76     "Taxation, interference with agriculture" Ibid: 104.

*Sweeping paper from the floor of the New York Stock Exchange after a day of heavy trading.*

p. 78    "Society may subsist . . . destroy it." Smith: 86.
p. 83    "He wanted economics to be realistic" Backhouse: 181.
p. 86    "one of the most important breakthroughs" Arnold: 5.
p. 86    "The modern world is built" *Economist*, 23 Dec. 1999.
p. 87    "create excessive speculation" Carney: 663.
p. 88    "declared the capital to be non-refundable" Neal, "Venture shares of the Dutch East India Company" in Geert and Rouwenhorst: 167.
p. 90    "Go for a business that any idiot" http://www.investopedia.com.
p. 92    "the most significant financial instruments" Arnold: 100.
p. 96    "In 2002 alone . . . over £7 billion." Ibid: 40–41.
p. 97    "the thought of ultimate loss" Quoted in Bishop: 18.
p. 98    "If past history was all" http://www.investopedia.com.
p. 99    "A state in which" Bannock, Baxter and Davis: 338.
p. 99    "the dangerous practice of stock-jobbing" Quoted in Mackay: 50.

CHAPTER 3 · STUDENT OF FINANCE

p. 103    "What is an investment?" Bishop: 145.
p. 107    "Although his efforts" Clarke: 233.
p. 110    "In all of these examples" Ibid: 225.
p. 110    "tipped the whole balance" Barnett: 263.
p. 111    "While Britain remained" Darwin: 131
p. 111    "it could only be a matter of time" Ibid: 133.
p. 114    "extremely friendly" Quoted in Darwin: 105
p. 114    "We have the material resources" Quoted in Hyam: xlix.
p. 114    "If we only pushed" Quoted in Hyam: 1.
p. 115    "I am not prepared to sacrifice" Quoted in Dutt; 37.
p. 116    "As the world moved out" Darwin: 136.
p. 116    "In 1970, British exports" Lipton and Firn: 19.
p. 118    "The men in this book" Holbrook: viii.
p. 118    "How much panache" Josephson: ix.
p. 120    "$552,520 on paper" Quoted in Holbrook: 227.
p. 121    "No other of the great money-lords" Josephson: 404.
p. 121    "a paradise for the entrepreneur" Ibid: vii.
p. 121    "whose population doubles" Ibid: 405.
p. 122    "In all the north land" Quoted in Leacock: 19.
p. 123    "There are no limits" Quoted in "Royal Homecoming" special issue of *Illustrated London News*, 24 Nov. 1951.
p. 123    "Canada is a place" Letter from Keynes to his sister, quoted in Skidelsky: 768.
p. 126    "Howe . . . opposed" Bliss: 457.

## CHAPTER 4 · INVESTING IN CANADA

p. 131    "Canada is a place" Letter from Keynes to his sister, quoted in Skidelsky: 768.

p. 140    "In survey after survey" Newman: 248.

p. 140    "We get up in the morning" Quoted in Newman: 23.

p. 141    "resembled nothing so much" Newman: 25.

p. 142    "Holt received his public elegy" Ibid: 44.

p. 142    "acquired the insensibility" Ibid: 54.

p. 143    "absurd, a railroad" Bliss: 293.

p. 144    " the entire CPR system" Newman: 75.

p. 145    "the inventor of a grasshopper killer" Ibid: 74.

p. 145    "the beer baron" Ibid: 223.

p. 145    "the free enterprise system" Ibid: 223.

p. 146    "Taylor assembled" Ibid: 231.

p. 147    " a special-situations company" Quoted in Newman: 241.

p. 147    "In each of its extensions" Newman: 241.

p. 148    "In its first ten years" Bliss: 467.

p. 148    "It's a question of judgement" Quoted in Bliss: 467.

p. 152    "The building on Place Ville-Marie" Bliss: 501.

p. 152    "The traditional branch manager" Ibid: 487.

## CHAPTER 5 · THE PAGURIAN STORY

p. 155    "Members of a species" *Globe and Mail*, 22 Oct. 1984.

p. 159    "Next to the Bible" Hackett: 59.

p. 160    "The book that time judges" Quoted in Hackett: 8.

p. 167    "1. What is the company's history?" Getty: 175–76.

p. 186    "As President Christopher Ondaatje" *Financial Post*, 31 May 1986.

p. 192    "I'm *least* proud" Quoted in David Olive, "In the skin of the scion", *Toronto Life*, Nov. 1989.

## CHAPTER 6 · WARNINGS FROM HISTORY

p. 193    "Money . . . has often been a cause" Mackay: xvi.

p. 194    "I certainly view" Ondaatje, *Woolf in Ceylon*: 21.

p. 194    "an empire that is more global" Soros, *Open Society*: 171.

p. 195    "At length corruption" Quoted in Mackay: 78.

p. 199    "The first direction . . . but cash." Glubb: 493.

p. 199    "from service to selfishness" Ibid: 494.

p. 199    "Amid a Babel of talk" Ibid: 496.

p. 199    "The citizens . . . will no longer" Ibid: 506.

p. 199    "The word 'celebrity'" Ibid: 499–500.

p. 200    "We have not drawn" Ibid: 502–03.

p. 200    "The empire analogy" Soros, *Open Society*: 171–72.

p. 203    "Imports exceeded exports"  Clarke: 12.

p. 204    "The fundamental trouble"  Quoted in Fraser: 391.

p. 207    "The creation of credit"  Duncan: 12–13.

p. 207    "the greatest economist"  Quoted in *The Times*, 28 Jan. 2006.

p. 208    "In 1980, it took . . . become worthless."  Bonner: 152–53.

p. 209    "Clearly, sustained low inflation"  Alan Greenspan's entire speech is available at http://www.federalreserve.gov/BOARDDOCS/SPEECHES/19961205.htm.

p. 211    "In today's electronic world"  Bonner: 271–72.

p. 211    "Money is increasingly an endogenous"  Lucarelli: 5.

p. 211    "Just as the interwar crisis"  Ibid: 163.

p. 214    "implicated virtually"  Fraser: 537.

p. 216    "direct ownership of stocks"  John C. Bogle, "Individual stockholder, R.I.P.", *Wall Street Journal*, 3 Oct. 2005.

p. 216    "Irrational exuberance really is"  Shiller: xii.

p. 216    "People will increasingly fear . . . bad outcomes."  Ibid: xv.

p. 220    "the belief that the system"  Soros, *Open Society*: 289.

p. 221    "We have not drawn"  Glubb: 502–03.

# BIBLIOGRAPHY

The bibliography lists only the major sources used in the research and writing of the book, including all directly quoted sources. Internet sources have not been included, with a few exceptions.

Arnold, Glen, *The Financial Times Guide to Investing*, London: FT Prentice Hall, 2004

Backhouse, Roger E., *The Penguin History of Economics*, London: Penguin, 2002

Bannock, Graham, R. E. Baxter and Evan Davis, *The Penguin Dictionary of Economics*, 7th edn, London: Penguin, 2003

Barnett, Correlli, *The Audit of War: The Illusion and Reality of Britain as a Great Nation*, London: Macmillan, 1986

Bell, Lilian A., *Papyrus, Tapa, Amate and Rice Paper: Papermaking in Africa, the Pacific, Latin America and Southeast Asia*, McMinnville (OR): Liliaceae Press, 1983

Best, Patricia and Ann Shortell, *The Brass Ring: Power, Influence and the Brascan Empire*, Toronto: Random House, 1988

Bishop, Matthew, *Essential Economics*, London: Economist Books, 2004

Bliss, Michael, *Northern Enterprise: Five Centuries of Canadian Business*, Toronto: McClelland and Stewart, 1987

Bloom, Jonathan M., *Paper Before Print: The History and Impact of Paper in the Islamic World*, New Haven (CT): Yale University Press, 2001

Bogle, John C., "Individual stockholder, R.I.P.", *Wall Street Journal*, 3 Oct. 2005: 16

Bonner, William with Addison Wiggin, *Financial Reckoning Day: Surviving the Soft Depression of the 21st Century*, Hoboken (NJ): John Wiley, 2003

Briggs, Asa and Peter Burke, *A Social History of the Media: From Gutenberg to the Internet*, Oxford: Polity Press, 2002

Burnham, Peter, *The Political Economy of Postwar Reconstruction*, London: Macmillan, 1989

Cairncross, Alec, *Years of Recovery: British Economic Policy 1945–51*, London: Methuen, 1985

Carney, William J., "Limited liability", http://encyclo.findlaw.com/5620book.pdf

Clarke, Peter, *Hope and Glory: Britain 1900–2000*, 2nd edn, London: Penguin, 2004

Collins, Nina L., *The Library in Alexandria and the Bible In Greek*, Leiden: Brill, 2000

Darwin, John, *Britain and Decolonisation: The Retreat from Empire in the Postwar World*, Basingstoke: Macmillan, 1988

Deacon, Richard, *A Biography of William Caxton: The First English Editor, Printer, Merchant and Translator*, London: Muller, 1976

Diringer, David, *The Book Before Printing: Ancient, Medieval and Oriental*, New York: Dover, 1982

Duncan, Richard, *The Dollar Crisis: Causes, Consequences, Cures*, Chichester: John Wiley, 2003

Dutt, Rajani Palme, *Britain's Crisis of Empire*, London: Lawrence and Wishart, 1949

Eisenstein, Elizabeth L., *The Printing Revolution in Early Modern Europe*, Cambridge: Cambridge University Press, 1983

Febvre, Lucien and Henri-Jean Martin, *The Coming of the Book: The Impact of Printing, 1450–1800*, (David Gerard trans.), London: Verso, 1990

Fraser, Steve, *Wall Street: A Cultural History*, London: Faber and Faber, 2005

Getty, J. Paul, *How To Be Rich*, London: W. H. Allen, 1966

Gittins, Susan, *Behind Closed Doors: The Rise and Fall of Canada's Edper Bronfman and Reichmann Empires*, Scarborough (Ontario): Prentice Hall, 1995

Glubb, John, "The fate of empires", *Blackwood's Magazine*, Dec. 1976: 484–511

Goetzmann, William N. and K Geert Rouwenhorst, eds, *The Origins of Value: The Financial Innovations That Created Modern Capital Markets*, New York: Oxford University Press, 2005

Goldsworthy, David, *Colonial Issues in British Politics 1945–1961: From 'Colonial Development' to 'Wind of Change'*, Oxford: Oxford University Press, 1971

Hackett, Alice Payne, *70 Years of Best Sellers 1895–1965*, New York: R. R. Bowker, 1967

Holbrook, Stewart H., *The Age of the Moguls*, London: Victor Gollancz, 1954

Hyam, Ronald, *The Labour Government and the End of Empire, 1945–1951, Part 1: High Policy and Administration*, London: HMSO, 1992

James, Lawrence, *The Rise and Fall of the British Empire*, London: Little, Brown, 1994

Josephson, Matthew, *The Robber Barons: The Great American Capitalists 1861–1901*, New York: Harcourt Brace, 1934

Krozewski, Gerold, *Money and the End of Empire: British International Economic Policy and the Colonies, 1947–58*, Basingstoke: Palgrave, 2001

Kurelek, William:
    *Kurelek's Canada*, Toronto: Canadian Heritage Library, 1975
    *The Last of the Arctic*, Toronto: Pagurian Press, 1976

Leacock, Stephen, *The Mariner of St. Malo: A Chronicle of the Voyages of Jacques Cartier*, Toronto: Glasgow, Brook, 1920

Lipton, Michael and John Firn, *The Erosion of a Relationship: India and Britain since 1960*, London: Oxford University Press, 1975

Lucarelli, Bill, *Monopoly Capitalism in Crisis*, Basingstoke: Palgrave Macmillan, 2004

McIntyre, W. David, *British Decolonization, 1946–1997: When, Why, and How Did the British Empire Fall?*, Basingstoke: Macmillan, 1998

Mackay, Charles, *Extraordinary Popular Delusions and the Madness of Crowds*, Ware (UK): Wordsworth Editions, 1995 (originally pubd in 1841)

MacLeod, Roy, ed., *The Library of Alexandria: Centre of Learning in the Ancient World*, London: I. B. Tauris, 2000

Man, John, *The Gutenberg Revolution: The Story of a Genius and an Invention That Changed the World*, London: Review, 2002

Middleton, Roger, *The British Economy Since 1945: Engaging with the Debate*, Basingstoke: Macmillan, 2000

Morley, Patricia, *Kurelek: A Biography*, Toronto: Macmillan, 1986

Narita, Kiyofusa, *A Life of Ts'ai Lung and Japanese Paper-Making*, Tokyo: Dainihon Press, 1966

Newman, Peter C., *Flame of Power: Intimate Profiles of Canada's Greatest Businessmen*, Toronto: Longmans, Green, 1959

Ondaatje, Christopher:
    *Fool's Gold: The First Million*, New York: Scribners, 1974 (under the pseudonym Simon Marawille)
    *The Prime Ministers of Canada, 1867–1967*, Toronto: Canyon Press, 1967
    *Woolf in Ceylon: An Imperial Journal in the Shadow of Leonard Woolf 1904–1911*, Toronto: HarperCollins, 2005

Ondaatje, Christopher and Gordon Currie, *Olympic Victory*, Toronto: Pagurian Press, 1967

Pixley, Jocelyn, *Emotions in Finance: Distrust and Uncertainty in Global Markets*, New York: Cambridge University Press, 2004

Robbins, L. C., *An Essay on the Nature and Significance of Economic Science*, 2nd edn, London: Macmillan, 1935

Robinson, Andrew, *The Story of Writing: Hieroglyphs, Alphabets and Pictograms*, London: Thames and Hudson, 1995

Ross, Alexander, *The Traders: Inside Canada's Stock Markets*, Toronto: Collins, 1984

Shiller, Robert J., *Irrational Exuberance*, 2nd edn, Princeton: Princeton University Press, 2005

Skidelsky, Robert, *John Maynard Keynes 1883–1946, Economist, Philosopher, Statesman*, London: Macmillan, 2003

Smith, Adam, *The Theory of Moral Sentiments*, (D. D. Raphael and A. L. Macfie eds), Oxford: Oxford University Press, 1976 (originally pubd in 1759–90)

Smith, Helena, "Capital of memory—famed ancient library of Alexandria inspires a modern version, Alexandrina Bibliotheca", *New Statesman*, 3 Sept. 2001

Soros, George:
    *The Crisis of Global Capitalism: Open Society Endangered*, London: Little, Brown, 1998
    *Open Society: Reforming Global Capitalism*, London: Little, Brown, 2000

Warner, J. Christopher, *Henry VIII's Divorce: Literature and the Politics of the Printing Press*, Woodbridge (UK): Boydell Press, 1998

White, Nicholas J., *Decolonisation: The British Experience Since 1945*, Harlow: Longman, 1999

# INDEX

Abbasids  46, 53
Alexander the Great  37, 38, 198
Alexandria, Library of  37–40
Amalfi  47
*amate*  31
American Resource Corporation  179
Amsterdam Exchange  89, 93
Andrew, Prince  23
Aquinas, Saint Thomas  67–68
Arabs  45–47
Argus Corporation  147–48, 169
Aristotle  37, 67
Art Gallery of Nova Scotia  15
Ashurbanipal  39
Athens  33, 35, 66
Attlee, Clement  105, 107
Augustine, Saint  67
Aztecs  54

Backhouse, Roger  66, 68, 71, 74, 77,
    83, 101
Baghdad  44, 45, 53, 199
Bank of England  58–59, 71, 75, 79,
    89, 110, 202
Barbon, Nicholas  74
Barnes, Robert  39
Barnett, Correlli  110
Bay Street (Toronto)  19, 22–23, 137,
    154, 158, 169, 170, 184
Beaverbrook, Lord  146, 152
Bell, Lilian  31
Bell Telephone (company)  136–37, 177
Benoit, Jehane  162, 163

Bentham, Jeremy  80
Berglund, Berndt  162
Berkshire Hathaway (company)  98
Berthelet, Thomas  57
Bevan, Aneurin  108, 109
Beveridge, William  109
Bevin, Ernest  106, 114, 115
Bible  39, 50–51, 56
Bibliotheca Alexandrina  38, 40
Bishop, Matthew  103
Black, Conrad  15
Black Death  68
Black Photo (company)  173–75, 177,
    178–79, 181
Blair, Tony  15
Bliss, Michael  126, 143, 152
Bloom, Jonathan  44–46, 53
Blundell's School  13, 15
Bogle, John  216
Bolsby, Clare E.  162
Bombay  70
Bonner, William  208, 211
Bonnycastle, Richard  22
Book of the Dead (Egyptian)  36
Bretton Woods  206, 212
Briggs, Asa  53, 57, 58
Bronfman family  24, 182–84, 189
Brookfield Asset Management
    (company)  24, 192
Brown, Gordon  207
Bruges  55
Buffett, Warren  90, 98, 99
Bulins, Valda, see Valda Ondaatje

Burke, Peter  53, 57, 58

Burns Brothers and Denton (company)
132, 136–37, 177

Burton, Sir Richard Francis  17

Butler, Rab  108

Caesar, Julius  39

Cai Lun, see Ts'ai Lun

Cairo  29, 45

Calcutta  70

Calgary  151, 181

Canadian Corporate Services
(company)  189

Canadian Express (company)  185

Canadian Pacific Railway  142–44,
148, 194

Capone, Al  122

Carnegie, Andrew  118, 128, 140

Carney, William  87

Cartier, Jacques  122

Cather, Willa  11

Catherine of Aragon  57

Caxton, William  55–56

cave paintings  29, 31

censorship of print  54–55, 57

Ceylon (Sri Lanka)  12, 14, 24–25,
27, 61, 62, 104, 113–14, 131,
148, 192, 193

Charles II (of England)  74

Chaucer, Geoffrey  29, 55

Chester Playhouse  15

Chicago  122

Chinese  33, 34, 40–45, 47, 48–50,
54, 58, 74, 211, 221

Chrétien, Jean  15

Churchill, Sir Winston  106, 112, 123

Clarke, Peter  106, 110, 203

Cleopatra  39

Clive, Robert  70

Cockwell, Jack  183, 184, 189

Coleridge, Samuel Taylor  26

Collins, Nina  39

Commonwealth of Nations  113–14,
115–16

Cromwell, Oliver  57

cuneiform script  32–33, 64–65

Currie, Gordon  164

Dalhousie University  15, 192

Damascus  45

Darwin, John  111, 116

Datini, Francesco di Marco  48

Deacon, Richard  55–56

Diefenbaker, John  153, 169

Dodd, David  173, 174, 181

Dominion Securities (company)  171

Duncan, Richard  207

Dunn, Sir James  145

Dutch East India Company  62–63, 70,
88–89

Eaton, Trevor  184

Edper Group (company)  182–84, 189

Eisenstein, Elizabeth  48

Elizabeth II (of Great Britain)  15

empires  62, 68, 70, 104, 106, 111–17,
193–95, 197–201, 221

Enfield Corporation  179, 181, 185

English East India Company  62–63,
69–71, 86, 89, 178, 194

Enron (company)  213–14

Fabriano 47

Febvre, Lucien 52

Federal Reserve Board 207–10

*Financial Post* newspaper 139, 148–49, 150, 153, 154, 186

financial securities, types of 89–95

FTSE index 96

Firn, John 116

Fleming, John 177, 181

*Fool's Gold* (Ondaatje) 20, 61, 164–65

Ford, Henry 119, 140

Franklin, Ed 169, 177

Fraser, Steven 204, 214

Fust, Johannes 50–52, 59

Gaitskell, Hugh 107–08

Gates, Bill 98

General Agreement on Tariffs and Trade 85, 201

Getty, J. Paul 165–69, 173, 181

Glass-Steagall Act 205

Glenthorne House 12

Glubb, Sir John 197–201, 211, 221

Goebbels, Joseph 55

Goetzmann, William 42, 61, 70

gold standard 203–04, 206, 208

Goldman Sachs (company) 214

Goldsmith, James 182

Gordon, Donald

Gordon-Walker, Patrick 114

Gournay, Vincent de 77

Grafton, Richard 56

Graham, Benjamin 173, 174, 181

Greenspan, Alan 207–11

Gutenberg, Johannes 42, 48–52, 55, 56, 59, 155, 173

Hackett, Alice Payne 159–60

Halifax 14

Hall, Charles 120

Harlequin Books (company) 161, 170–71, 182

Hart, James 160, 162

Harun ar-Rashid 46

Hees International (company) 183–85, 189

Heine, Heinrich 54

Hemingway, Ernest 18

*Hemingway in Africa* (Ondaatje) 18

Henry VIII (of England) 57

Hesiod 66

hieroglyphic writing 33, 54

Hogarth, William 196

Holbrook, Stewart 118–19

Holt, Sir Herbert 140–42, 143, 152

Homer 66

Hospital for Sick Children (Toronto) 15

Ho Ti 40–41

Howe, C. D. 124–25, 126–27, 134

Hudson's Bay Company 123, 142

Hume, David 75, 76

Hutcheson, Francis 76

Hutchison, Bruce 159

*Hypnerotomachia Poliphili* 53–54

*incunabula* 52, 53

International Monetary Fund 85, 200, 201, 206, 213, 220

International Pagurian, see Pagurian Corporation

Jacomb, Robert  100
Jennison, Clark  147
Jevons, William  82
Josephson, Matthew  118–19
*Journey to the Source of the Nile*
    (Ondaatje)  18

Kaufman, Henry  214
Keller, Saxon  59
Keynes, John Maynard  17, 83–84,
    97, 105, 109, 112, 123, 131, 204
Khomeini, Ayatollah  55
King, Gregory  71
King, Mackenzie  126, 134, 135
Knossos  33
Koran  68
Korthals, Robert W.  184
Kurelek, William  22, 161–62

laissez faire economics  77–78
Lakefield College School  15
Laurier, Wilfrid  124
Law, John  75
Lend-Lease  105, 124
*Leopard in the Afternoon* (Ondaatje)
    192
L'Estrange, Sir Roger  58
limited liability companies  86–87,
    117
Linear B script  33
Lipton, Michael  116
Livermore, Jesse  96, 99
Locke, John  71, 72–74
Loewen, Charles  22, 153–54,
    156, 169

Loewen Ondaatje McCutcheon
    (company)  156, 161, 165, 169–72,
    175, 185, 212
London School of Economics  28, 63,
    104, 149
London Stock Exchange  89, 95–96
Long Term Capital Management
    (company)  209
Louis XIV (of France)  75, 77
Love, Philip  120
Lucarelli, Bill  211–12
Luther, Martin  52
Lynch, Peter  90

McCutcheon, Frederick C.  22,
    156, 169
Macdonald, Sir John A.  157
Machiavelli, Niccolò  69
Mackay, Charles  193, 195
Maclean Hunter (company)  137–38,
    148, 154
MacLeod, Roy  38
Macmillan, Harold  108
Madras  70
Mainz  48–52, 155
Malthus, Thomas  80
Man, John  48, 50
Mandeville, Bernard  76
*The Man-Eater of Punanai* (Ondaatje)
    14
Marawille, Simon (pseudonym of
    Christopher Ondaatje), see *Fool's
    Gold*
Marco Polo  47
Markowitz, Harry  212
Marshall, Alfred  82–83

Marshall Plan 115, 135

Martin, Henri-Jean 52

Marvell, Andrew 58

Marx, Karl 81

Massey College 192

Mayas 54

Mellon, Andrew 119–20, 121

mercantilism 69, 74, 78

Mill, John Stuart 87

Montreal 20, 124, 137–38, 140, 145, 149, 152, 153, 171

Montreal Museum of Fine Arts 143

*Montrealer* magazine 137–38, 153

Moorish rule 47, 68

Morgan, J. P. 96–97, 120–21, 128, 205

Muir, James 152

Mun, Thomas 71

Naess, Arne 186–87

National Bank of India 62, 103–04, 110, 116, 194

National Health Service 106, 108, 109, 202

National Portrait Gallery 14, 192

Neal, Larry 88–89

New York Stock Exchange 95–96, 222

Newman, Peter C. 139–48

Newton, Sir Isaac 71, 74

Nietzsche, Friedrich 16

Nile, River 18, 35

Nixon, Richard 40

Nuremberg 47

Odlum, Floyd 147

Ogilby, John 58

oil and gas industry 127, 151, 177, 180–81

Olive, David 24

Olympic Games (Innsbruck, 1964) 21, 164

*Olympic Victory* (Currie and Ondaatje) 164, 192

Ondaatje, David 21, 138

Ondaatje, Doris 25, 61–62

Ondaatje, Jans (now Jans Ondaatje Rolls) 21, 153

Ondaatje, Mervyn 25, 27, 61, 62, 192

Ondaatje, Sarah 21, 149

Ondaatje, Valda 21, 26, 138

oracle-bone inscriptions 33–34

Orwell, George 24

Osaka 94

Ottawa 146

Pagurian Corporation 22, 24, 150, 155–92

Pagurian Press, see Pagurian Corporation

*Pagurus marshi* (hermit crab) 22, 155

paper: definition of 29; invention of 40–41

paper money 42–44, 47, 58–60, 75, 120, 208, 211

papyrus 29, 30, 33–38, 45

Patino family 182–85

Pearson, Lester B. 157

Pearson College 15, 192

Pei, I. M. 152

Peisistratus 38

Petty, William 71

physiocrats 76–77, 78

Pinchart-Deny, Christian 171
Pi Sheng 48
Pitfield Mackay Ross (company)
    153–54, 156, 165, 169, 170
*Plant Administration and Engineering*
    magazine 138, 149
Plato 66
Ponzi, Charles 214
Pope, Alexander 195
Potts, D. T. 32
Price, Tim 184
*Prime Ministers of Canada,*
    *1867–1967, The* (Ondaatje) 129,
    157–59, 162, 192
printing, invention of 48–50
Ptolemy dynasty 37, 39

Quesnay, François 76

Rand, Ayn 207
Ricardo, David 80–82, 202
Robbins, Lionel 63, 65
Robinson, Andrew 32
Rockefeller, John D. 118, 128
Roman, Stephen 128–29, 151, 158
Roosevelt, Franklin Delano 112,
    204–05
Ross, Diana 23, 186–87
Rouwenhorst, Geert 42, 61, 70
Royal Bank of Canada 141, 152
Royal Geographical Society 15, 192
Royal Ontario Museum 15
Royal Society 71
Rushdie, Salman 55

St Lawrence Seaway 145, 150–51
Samarkand 44–45
Saqqara 29
Sarbanes-Oxley Act 215
Saumarez Smith, Charles 14
Scribner, Charles 163
Securities and Exchange Commission
    205
Selborne, Lord 18
Senanayake, D. S. 114
Shakespeare, William 56
Shang dynasty 34
Shiller, Robert 212, 213, 216–17, 218
Shotoku, Empress 41
Signoret, Simone 26
Silk Road 41–42, 44
Sloane Square 12, 185
Smith, Adam 77–79, 82, 87, 101, 126
Smith, Donald, see Lord Strathcona
Smith, Sir Thomas 69
Solon 66
Somerset County Cricket Club 15
Song dynasty 42, 43–44, 74
Soros, George 95, 194, 200, 218–21
South Sea Bubble (and Company)
    99–100, 195–96, 217
Speke, John Hanning 17
Spencer, Herbert 13
Spenser, Edmund 56
Steinberg, Saul 122
Steuart, Sir James 77
Strathcona, Lord 142–43, 152
Stromer, Ulmann 47
*Style* magazine 138
Sumerians 32
Surat 70

Talas, battle of 44
Tang dynasty 4
*tapa* 31
Taylor, Edward Plunket 145–48, 169
T'eng, Dowager Empress 41
Thatcher, Margaret 110
Theophilus 39
Thornton, Henry 80
Toronto 14, 20, 22, 28, 131, 149, 155, 158, 161, 163
Toronto Dominion Bank 184
*Toronto Star* newspaper 171, 182
Toronto Stock Exchange 156, 171, 173, 189
Trudeau, Pierre 23, 153
Ts'ai Lun 40–42, 44, 45, 48
tulipmania 94
Turfan 41

Vancouver 171
Vanderbilt, Cornelius 118
Vanguard (company) 216
Van Horne, Sir William 143–45
Velcro 165, 186
vellum 37, 50
Venice 53, 68
VOC, see Dutch East India Company
von Glahn, Richard 42, 43

Wall Street 96, 118, 120, 121, 137, 203, 204, 205, 212
Walpole, Sir Robert 99, 100, 217
Walras, Léon 82
Warka 32, 33

Warner, Christopher 57
wars:
    English Civil War 57
    First World War 59, 83, 105, 203
    Iraq War 210
    Korean War 107, 110, 127, 135
    Second World War 59, 84, 105, 111, 123, 133, 201, 206
    Seven Years War 59
    Vietnam War 170, 206
Washington Loan Agreement 105, 112, 125
Webster, Donald C. 22
Westdale Oil and Gas (company) 177, 181
Weston, Galen and Hilary 15
White, Mike 131–32
William III (of Great Britain) 59, 71, 89
Wilson, Trevor 23
Woolf, Leonard 194
*Woolf in Ceylon* (Ondaatje) 194
Worde, Winkyn de 57
World Bank 85, 201, 206, 213
World Trade Organisation 85, 213
WorldCom (company) 213
writing, origins of 29, 31–33

Xenophon 66
Xerxes 38

Zeckendorf, William 152
Ziyad ibn Salih 44
Zurich 56